ELGAR
In Love

© Kevin Allen 2000

First Published July 2000

Elgar in Love : Vera Hockman and the Third Symphony.

ISBN 0 - 9531227 - 2 - 7

Published by the author at 23, Benbow Close, Malvern Wells,
Worcs, UK. WR14 4JJ

Printed in England by
Aldine Press Limited,
Barnards Green Road,
Malvern,
Worcs.
WR14 3NB

Further copies may be obtained from the author at £11.85 inc. p & p

In memory of Carice Elgar Blake

ELGAR IN LOVE

VERA HOCKMAN AND THE THIRD SYMPHONY

Kevin Allen

The Young Vera

FOREWORD

By Michael Kennedy, CBE

When audiences listen to Anthony Payne's elaboration of the sketches of Elgar's Third Symphony, I think it is fair to say that the moment when they think "Ah! this is Elgar!" is at the 27th bar of the score when the *cantabile* second subject is first heard, a tender, yearning, passionate melody of the type he would formerly have described as "Windflowerish." We know that the very opening of the work is fully scored by Elgar, and very characteristic it is, but this second theme is the Elgar we have known from the *Woodland Interlude*, the *Adagio* of the First Symphony, the second subject of the Violin Concerto and the *Dream Interlude* in Falstaff. (Incidentally, "elaboration" seems to me to be a prosaic word for what Mr Payne has achieved. Ignition would be better, for he has acted as Prometheus to these sketches which have lain in the British Library for over half a century.) This theme is clearly marked in the sketches as 'V. H.'s own theme.' It has been known for some time that V. H. was Vera Hockman, the young Jewish semi-professional violinist with whom Elgar had a close friendship in the last two and a quarter years of his life. But it is only now, with Kevin Allen's book, the result of scrupulous research, that we are able to understand how close that friendship was and that it was almost certainly the cause of the sudden flaring-up of his creative fire after a decade of sterility. The tragedy is that it coincided with the onset of his last illness and failing physical powers. Alive creatively again, he also knew he had little time left and he tried to cram in too much, switching from symphony to opera and even contemplating the remnants of the piano concerto which an earlier muse, Alice Stuart Wortley, had inspired.

For Elgar needed muses always, that is inescapable. First Helen Weaver, then unknown inspirers in Scotland and France, Rosa Burley, Dorabella, Alice Stuart Wortley, Julia Worthington, perhaps Florence Norbury and Adela Schuster, and above them all Alice Elgar herself, who ordered his life, kept him at his desk, badgered his publishers and understood that she was the immovable rock in his life wherever else his fancy might roam for more poetic inspiration. But once Alice had gone, what then ? With no one to make him work, he all too easily frittered his time away in more trivial pursuits than music, except for conducting it and making gramophone records. It was better fun to go to the races, to walk with the dogs around the haunts of his youth, to buy new cars, to create his own mythology, to talk to actors in his club and to expand a most curious friendship (as Mr Allen shows us) with Bernard Shaw of which we may be sure Alice would have disapproved. Friendship between the socialist Shaw and the Edward Elgar who at the same time resigned from the Athenaeum when the first Socialist Prime Minister, Ramsay MacDonald, was elected a member! This kind of existence did not call for a muse. He never even seems to have considered re-marriage and slipped easily into the way of life of a confirmed bachelor.

And then came that Croydon rehearsal of *The Dream of Gerontius* on 7 November 1931 at which his eyes alighted on Vera Hockman in the violin section. Her own account of that occasion and of what followed, with Mr Allen's own narrative of events, ensures that this book contributes a major piece of evidence towards not only the gestation of the Third Symphony but to the chronicling of the last years of the composer's life. Mr Allen tells us how Mrs Hockman tried to publish her memories many years ago but was rebuffed by that strain of English puritanism which insists that great men must not be seen to be human. Of course, the sight of old men infatuated with young women is one from which guardians of the flame wish to shield the rest of us. But Mrs Hockman's account makes it very obvious that this was no senile infatuation. Just when she wrote down her memories is not clear, but it would seem that she must have made notes, perhaps in a diary, at the time, because her account of Elgar's conversation vividly captures the Elgar we know from his letters to others. His touching and humorous relationship with her daughter Dulcie is *echt*-Elgar and can be compared with the postcards he used to send to his daughter Carice and the letters he wrote to Dorabella.

Today the questions that many would ask are 'Did they go to bed together?', 'Did they have sex?' (The latter such an unromantic description of making love!) The inquisitive will find no answers here. Mrs Hockman belonged to a generation which did not advertise its private life and, although they had plenty of opportunity, we are left to draw what conclusions we like from the change from 'Dear Mrs Hockman' to 'Sweetest and dearest' and Elgar's description of Vera as 'my mother, my child, my lover and my friend.' His gift to her of the sketches of the Violin Sonata and of the *Hyperion* that belonged to his mother signifies something much deeper than a "little flutter," as some have minimised this relationship. To associate Vera with his music and with the days of his boyhood with his mother, one of the few who believed in him, tells us more about his feelings for her than we would learn from any sexual history (which might after all only be a 'little flutter.') It is significant that Carice Elgar Blake liked and befriended Vera. She obviously knew that her father was not being a silly old man and if her friendship with Vera also served as a cloak against prying eyes where Elgar and Vera were concerned, that was fine. I was told that Carice was fearful that if they married – which would have been impossible because of the continued existence of Mr Hockman – her father's will would be altered. But he could have altered it anyway. It's more likely that she was perturbed about the Roman Catholic-Jewish complication.

Mr Allen's book is to be welcomed also because it deals frankly with Carice herself, a shadowy figure in most biographies of her father (as she would have wished). As a child, she was sacrificed by her mother on the altar of Elgar's career.

If a rehearsal coincided with an event in Carice's life, such as her confirmation, the rehearsal won every time. It is surprising that Elgar, who loved Carice, did not put his foot down on her behalf. She told me on one occasion that she thought her mother had been stupid and wrong in keeping certain people, such as Ernest Newman, away from Elgar – in Newman's case simply because he had dared to criticise the last two oratorios. I have always thought that it indicated what a terrifying matriarch Alice must have been that Elgar, who adored dogs, never had one during their marriage because Alice didn't like them (they may have had one, briefly, I believe). He and Carice certainly made up for it after Alice's death!

There are poignant reminders in this book, too, of how out of fashion Elgar was in some circles between 1920 and his death. The flattery he received from Shaw must have been one big reason for their friendship. It is reassuring to read of the ovations he received when he conducted the Second Symphony at the Proms in October 1930 and 1931. But whatever audiences felt (and even so his 70th birthday concert was poorly attended in 1927), the agenda was set by some academics like E. J. Dent, of whom Elgar had always been suspicious and hostile, and intellectuals like the Sitwells. We may also attribute to the influence of another composer, Frank Bridge, the priggishly stupid reaction of the 16-year-old Benjamin Britten. To that extent, the influence of Shaw on Sir John Reith of the BBC regarding the commissioning of the Third Symphony remains a beacon at a dark time. It is all the more distressing, therefore, to learn from Mr Allen of Shaw's shabby conduct over the £1,000 he lent to Elgar and of his disparaging remarks about his friend after his death. But that, alas, is the way of the world.

It is also the way of the world, thank goodness, that good-hearted, kindly, simple folk like Kathleen Harrison exist. Her account of Elgar's last days in the nursing-home and at Marl Bank will bring a tear to many eyes besides mine.

Michael Kennedy
April, 2000

By the same author :

Elgar the Cyclist

August Jaeger: Portrait of Nimrod (Ashgate Press)

CONTENTS

		Page
Foreword by Michael Kennedy … … … … … … … … … … … … …		v
Preface and Acknowledgements … … … … … … … … … … … …		x
List of Illustrations … … … … … … … … … … … … … … … … …		xii
Introduction:	The Courage to Defy Convention … … … … … … … …	1
Chapter 1	The Story of November 7th, 1931 … … … … … … … …	20
Chapter 2	V. H.'s own Theme … … … … … … … … … … … … …	64
Chapter 3	Life Goes On … … … … … … … … … … … … … … …	102
Appendix	*'You'll Never Leave Me, Will You?'* … … … … … … …	130
Notes	… …	135
Index	… …	145

PREFACE AND ACKNOWLEDGMENTS

Elgar's relationship with Vera Hockman has been public knowledge since 1984, when she was mentioned in two books published that year by Jerrold Northrop Moore, *Spirit of England* and *Edward Elgar, A Creative Life.* The former acknowledged the influence of her friendship on Elgar's undertaking of the ill-fated Third Symphony project after 'more than a dozen years away from major composition,' and referred specifically to the second main theme of its first movement, lyrical music which she inspired. The latter quoted passages from Vera's two reminiscences of the composer, *The Story of November 7th, 1931* and *Elgar and Poetry,* and went on to affirm her importance: '. . . perhaps for the first time since Alice's death he was aware of a woman who might stand between him and the world.' The point could not have been better put.

Michael Kennedy too has made frequent mention of Vera in various writings and broadcasts, and in the third edition of his *Portrait of Elgar* (1987). But one may be forgiven for wondering why her place in Elgar's life and work has remained so little known to a wider public. It is perfectly evident that various of the composer's friends who produced documentary accounts covering the latter part of his life and who must have known and met Vera, seem to have studiously avoided making any mention of her at all. Today we tend to find this kind of discretion unnecessary if not somewhat conspiratorial, but such friends must have understandably felt that in seeking to minimise knowledge of Elgar's relationship with Vera because of the danger of prurient comment, they were acting in his best interests. It was not the only sacrifice made on Elgar's behalf on the altar of those middle-class standards of behaviour and good taste which seem to have simultaneously attracted and repelled him throughout his life, further penalties of his English environment. As I have tried to show, and despite the received wisdom, Elgar never made a more determined intellectual effort to discard those standards than during the twenties, the period leading up to his first meeting with Vera. And if, as T. E. Lawrence said, Elgar's failure to complete the Third Symphony was a tragedy, so too perhaps was the existence of the complex of factors, circumstantial and cultural, which made a closer union between composer and muse out of the question.

Times have changed, but even so, and amid all the massive media coverage of the *Sketches for Elgar's Symphony No. 3, elaborated by Anthony Payne,* Vera's very existence, to say nothing of her rôle in the work, continues to be overlooked. The interval feature mounted for the televised 1998 Proms performance of the Symphony, for example, purported to offer an account of its creative origins, but made no mention of Vera at all. Instead, in a classic piece of instant media myth-making, the entire credit for the work was given to Bernard Shaw. But under the very noses of various distinguished commentators, the programme also included archive film of Vera and Elgar together which virtually shouts out to us of the quality of communication between them; it went unremarked.

Seldom can the existence of a major influence on the life and work of a great composer have been so ignored. There would seem every reason to argue that it is high time that Vera's memories, so full of her own warmth and honesty, were published in full. One is tempted to claim that they represent perhaps the last great Elgarian documentary discovery to be made. Without them our knowledge and understanding of Elgar, full as they are in so many ways, would be less than complete. They will offer scholars rich fields of further investigation.

The question arises of the inevitable invasion of privacy such publication entails, especially with documents which are so personal and intimate. But there is every sign that Vera wanted her Elgarian reminiscences to be known. Present-day family members, who have given every encouragement to this project, tell me that her writings were originally produced especially to share with understanding friends. There is also the evidence of her approaches to Vaughan Williams and Steuart Wilson, asking for help in efforts to have them published for the benefit of a wider audience. Other documents, particularly the letters between Elgar and Vera, have been destroyed, thus perforce respecting privacy and most happily removing any possible qualms of conscience for both researcher and reader.

What follows is an effort to present, in addition to her own writings, almost every other documentary item concerning Vera that I have been able to find; this has led me to include something which may not be without interest of the little-known and often difficult life of one of her friends, the composer's daughter, Carice Elgar Blake. Further, I have tried to see Elgar and Vera in the context of the whole of the last phase of his life after Alice's death, and in the context too of the story of the Third Symphony. Here it has been possible to offer some documentary evidence which should clear up the often expressed puzzlement over W. H. Reed's publication of the sketches. I have made a point, too, of introducing some Shaw material which I have not yet seen included in any discussion of his relations with Elgar. If I have tended perhaps to be somewhat hard on one referred to by Winston Churchill as 'this unique and double-headed chameleon,' then I plead guilty to indulging in exaggeration the better to make a point; but I do feel that there is a certain imbalance to be redressed here. Finally, I have been unable to resist an opportunity of including some previously unpublished letters to Vera from another great English composer whose music and character she loved, Ralph Vaughan Williams.

In 1979, through a family contact, a typescript copy of Vera's *Story of November 7th, 1931* was read by Sir David Willcocks, then Director of the Royal College of Music. He asked that a copy be lodged in the College Library and noted that he had been ' . . . fascinated to read the . . . account of Elgar's little flutter. Very romantic! It would make a good film.' While it is my aim in what follows to suggest that the relationship between Edward Elgar and Vera Hockman was in fact something more than a 'little flutter,' there can be little disagreement that it would make a good film. I hope I may be forgiven for suggesting that it would certainly make a better film than a recent effort misleadingly titled *Elgar's Last Muse*, and that it would provide an account of Elgar and Vera far more genuine and dignified than that offered in David Pownall's radio play, *Elgar's Third*. After all, as George Bernard Shaw himself said in one of his early novels, 'the chief objection to fictitious romance is that it is seldom so romantic as the truth.'

*

My first thanks are due to those of Vera Hockman's relatives and descendants I have been able to meet and who have generously helped with the provision of documentary material, memories, information, and advice. I am particularly grateful to Vera's adopted daughter, Nina Driver, for her most kind loan of the original handwritten copy of *The Story of November 7th, 1931* together with other material including the Elgar Third Symphony sketches and the letters of Ralph Vaughan Williams published herein.

I wish also to record my thanks to Neil Somerville of the BBC Written Archives Centre at Caversham Park, Dr Jenny Doctor of the Britten-Pears Library, Aldeburgh, Dr Peter Horton of the Royal College of Music Library, Steve Roud and Margaret Mumford of the Local Studies Library at Croydon Central Library, Nicholas Williams of the *Musical Times* and Katharine Ellis of *Music & Letters*, The Parkinson's Disease Society, Hugh Cobbe FSA, Sir David Willcocks, Ursula Vaughan Williams, Ron Taylor, Geoffrey Hodgkins, Editor of the *Elgar Society Journal,* and Sylvia Disley.

It has been a particular pleasure to make contact with Ethel Kirby, who celebrated her centenary this year, and who kindly provided the portrait photograph of her late husband. I am privileged to be able to include also photographs of Elgar, Shaw, Vaughan Williams and others at various Three Choirs Festivals, taken from the private collection of Wynne Tucker, past Secretary of the Worcester Festival Choral Society, to whom I offer my warmest thanks. It is another pleasure to acknowledge my debt to Raymond Monk for permission to include the photographs of Carice Elgar Blake and the letter of T. E. Lawrence in his possession, and for much other help and encouragement besides. I am most grateful also to Melanie Weatherly, Cathie Sloan and Chris Bennett for permission to reproduce various photographs held by the Elgar Birthplace Museum and for the facilities afforded me to publish extracts from the newspaper cuttings books and from the diary of Carice Elgar Blake. I would also like to acknowledge gratefully the kind permission of the Birthplace to publish stills from Harold Brooke's film of Elgar, Vera and Carice at Marl Bank. I am most grateful to Michael Kennedy for agreeing to write a Foreword to this book, and for much kind help with the typescript.

Any omission of copyright acknowledgement is regretted and will be rectified in future editions.

LIST OF ILLUSTRATIONS

Front cover Elgar and Vera at Marl Bank, Friday 9th September 1932, together with Carice and the dogs.

Frontispiece The young Vera.

Between pages 48 and 63

Elgar, Billy Reed and Alan Kirby at Croydon, 7th November 1931

Alan Kirby

Croydon Baths Hall

Croydon High Street with Grant's on the right

The Shirley Park Hotel, formerly Shirley House

Dulcie and her Song

Two pages from Vera's *Pageant of English Poetry*, with Elgar's markings

'In remembrance Croydon 1931'

A message from Hyperion

Vera's house, Robin Hill

Vera with her children, mother and grandparents

Two portrait studies of Carice

Elgar arriving with Carice for her wedding at St. James's Church, Spanish Place, London on 16th January 1922

Carice and Sam Blake on their honeymoon

Between pages 88 and 101

'Love to Vera from Billy'

Dulcie's joke score

Elgar at the Hereford Festival, 1933

Elgar arriving at the cathedral, Worcester Festival 1932

'Will never be finished?' Two pages of Third Symphony sketches given to Vera, including the '1st sketch of V. H.'s own theme'

Elgar with the Menuhin family in Paris, 30th May 1933

Vera and friend at the Hereford Festival, 1933, with Elgar and Shaw

Elgar in conversation with the Shaws, Worcester Festival 1932

GBS and Charlotte, Gloucester Festival 1934

Carice and motor car

A letter of condolence from Lawrence of Arabia

Billy Reed conducting the brass chorales from the cathedral tower, Worcester Festival 1938

Ivor and Wulstan Atkins, Worcester Festival 1935

LIST   OF   ILLUSTRATIONS (CONTINUED)

Between pages 122 and 129

Vera with her granddaughter Marion and adopted daughter Nina, together with Dulcie's husband's mother, c. 1945

Vera, Dulcie and Marion in the garden at Robin Hill

A letter from 'Uncle Ralph'

Railway pass for a composer

V. W. at the Hereford Festival, 1933

V. W. and Percy Hull at the Worcester Festival, 1932

Don Cheeseman at rehearsal

'They all got to know.' Elgar's funeral, a newspaper photograph

AS YOU CAME FROM THE HOLY LAND

As you came from the holy land
    Of Walsinghame,
Met you not with my true love
    By the way as you came?

How shall I know your true love,
    That have met many one
As I went to the holy land,
    That have come, that have gone?

She is neither white nor brown,
    But as the heavens fair,
There is none hath a form so divine
    In the earth of the air.

Such an one did I meet, good sir,
    Such an angel-like face,
Who like a queen, like a nymph, did appear
    By her gait, by her grace.

She hath left me here all alone,
    All alone as unknown,
Who sometimes did me lead with herself,
    And me loved as her own.

What's the cause that she leaves you alone
    And a new way doth take,
Who loved you once as her own,
    And her joy did you make?

I have loved her all my youth,
    But now old as you see;
Love likes not the falling fruit
    From the withered tree.

Know that Love is a careless child,
And forgets promise past;
He is blind, he is deaf when he list
And in faith never fast.

His desire is a dureless content
And a trustless joy;
He is won with a world of despair
And is lost with a toy.

Of womenkind such indeed is the love
Or the word love abused,
Under which many childish desires
And conceits are excused.

But true love is a durable fire
In the mind ever burning;
Never sick, never old, never dead,
From itself never turning.

Sir Walter Ralegh

Introduction: The Courage to Defy Convention

The mind bold and independent
The purpose free . . .

Cardinal Newman

Elgar's extended period of creative near-sterility after the death of his wife on 7th April, 1920 is a familiar story. 'All I have done was owing to her and I am at present a sad and broken man,' wrote Elgar to Walford Davies in the aftermath of the funeral. For part of that summer he retreated to Brinkwells, the remote Sussex cottage surrounded by woods where he had composed the Cello Concerto and much of his chamber music. He knew that a chapter in his life was closed and felt that his creative life was over, writing to his friend Sidney Colvin: '. . . the old artistic 'striving' world exists for me no more . . . Inscrutable nature goes on just the same – young larks, six, in a nest on the lawn & many other birds; nightingales sing; but I miss the littlest gentlest presence & I cannot go on.' That presence had been essential to his creative work, and it seemed to Elgar that there could never be any replacement or substitute. A year later he again wrote to Colvin from the cottage: 'I have tried to take up the old life but it will not do and so there's an end. I feel like these woods all aglow – a spark wd start a flame – but no human spark comes.' Only with hindsight can we now see that this low point was not an end, but rather the beginning of a slow journey to a new creative urge and a new relationship.

By the time of that bereavement Julia Worthington, the gracious American lady of whom both Elgars had been so fond, was dead, and he had deliberately closed off relationships with other admiring women who had encouraged him in past years, such as Dora Penny and Rosa Burley. A dignified friendship continued with Alice Stuart Wortley, the 'Windflower' of the Violin Concerto, but it was now devoid of any inspirational fire. During the coming years, Elgar would show passing interest in several women, mainly younger and musical, and various women would set their caps at him. He had always been attractive to women and deeply susceptible to feminine influence, but the 'human spark' that would reignite the creative flame seemed nowhere on the immediate horizon. With the return of Brinkwells to its official tenant, the sale of Severn House and the emerging new spirit of the twenties, Elgar came to feel that the whole of his past life was being wiped out and that his music had vanished. He became not merely lonely and unhappy but desperate, more desperate perhaps than has been suspected. Sometimes his unhappiness showed in the most basic of ways, through bad temper and petty rudeness. Annoyed by an over-lengthy introduction by a local worthy as he was waiting to conduct a performance of *The Apostles* at Harlech in 1924, for example, Elgar turned to him and said, "Shut up, you fool," and raised his baton. There are various other such incidents, 'stories about Elgar that make you cringe,' as one of his biographers has said.

He restlessly sought escape in a variety of ways; as the country gentleman devoted to dogs and horseracing; as the book-loving scholar penning learned articles for the *Times Literary Supplement* from the libraries of his London clubs; as the amateur scientist delighting in images discovered through the lens of his microscope; and as an avid theatre and cinema-goer. Somewhat unpredictably, he undertook, too, a six-week cruise to South America and along the Amazon to Manaos. He remained close to several old friends, mostly male, and saw a good deal of his Worcestershire relatives and his daughter Carice, at least until her marriage in 1922. Musical activities did continue, as he accepted frequent invitations to conduct and record his music; such opportunities provided income and helped to reassure him that his music was wanted. But when, ageing and white-haired, he appeared on the platform year after year to conduct at the Three Choirs Festivals, Constant Lambert said it was as if one of the great classical figures of the past was somehow making a reappearance.

There was little enough new music from his pen during the whole of the twenties, and a list of it makes sad and all too brief reading. During ten years Elgar produced his Bach and Handel orchestrations, and arranged orchestral accompaniments to three Motets. He wrote six partsongs, a *Civic Fanfare* for the opening of the 1927 Hereford Festival, some potboilers for the Wembley Exhibition, a carillon obbligato for *Land of Hope and Glory*, incidental music for B. P. Matthews' *Beau Brummel*, and Laurence Binyon's *Arthur.* This latter Elgar took some particular trouble over and it contains much memorable music. But Alice stood behind it, for in writing hesitantly to Binyon over accepting the commission the composer remembered 'my wife loved your things.'

*

But together with Elgar's creative lethargy at this time there seemed to develop a new unconventionality of thought and behaviour, often deliberately and somewhat theatrically expressed when among friends and strongly contrasting with the bluff country gentleman image that he did so much to cultivate. Perhaps it was part of the Pantheism some critics have heard in the chamber music of Brinkwells and its glowing woods, although this is traceable much further back in Elgar's music, to the *Woodland Interlude* from *Caractacus*, for example, originally sketched in 1887. Basil Maine, Elgar's first major biographer, recounted an incident:

> . . . when the composer and he were the guests of Dr. C. Lee Williams at the Gloucester Club for the week of the Three Choirs' Meeting. At breakfast one morning Elgar produced his pocket-book, took from it a crumpled piece of paper and asked his fellow-guest to read out aloud what

was printed there. It was a quotation from Walt Whitman. To an audience consisting of the composer, Harold Brooke of Novello's and a waiter who was both astonished at what he heard and grieved that the guests should be neglecting the fried bacon and mushrooms which had just been brought in, these words were declaimed:

I think I could turn and live with animals, they are so placid and self-contained;
They do not sweat and whine about their condition;
They do not lie awake in the dark and weep for their sins;
They do not make me sick discussing their duty to God;
Not one is dissatisfied – not one is demented with the mania of owning things;
Not one kneels to another, nor to his kind that lived thousands of years ago;
Not one is respectable or industrious over the whole earth.

"That's my philosopy," said Elgar. At that moment, Dr. Lee Williams came in to greet his guests. He had overheard the last words of the reading.
"Have I interrupted the First Lesson?" he asked.
"Lee Williams would appreciate this," said Elgar. "Would you read it again?"
"You'll have to speak up," the host said, "I'm a little deaf." So once more, and rather louder, the passage was declaimed. The words were used later for the composer's private Christmas card, the most unconventional greeting, surely, that was ever sent by man to man at the season of goodwill.

Some years before, Elgar had accepted an invitation to spend a few days with his childhood friend Hubert Leicester at Worcester and his son Philip made notes of various after-dinner conversations. It might seem that, privately, the composer was anxious to cast off the repressions of years:

. . . he talked of the recent burglary at his house at Hampstead & his police court experiences connected with it. Said that he usually sympathised with the criminals – ' they are the only poets in these days.' – Young man on trial for seducing a girl of 17 who ran away with him from an unhappy home, got 12 months, & girl wept in court. E. said we were a curious nation. Our classical system of education caused hundreds of respectable gentlemen to spend their lives teaching thousands of school boys the pagan poets' theories of *love* – they wrote nothing about marriage – 'and when two young people have the courage to defy convention & follow the poets to find perfect bliss, you send the boy to gaol & the girl home to her parents.' He spoke jestingly but I could see he was half in earnest.

3

Family members became used to some merciless teasing on religious matters. During a conversation on the subject of life after death, Elgar was asked if he had considered what he would like to happen to him. After some pondering he replied: 'Up for climate, down for company.' And on being asked by a well-meaning elderly Catholic relative on how he was getting on with his false teeth, which he invariably forgot to wear, the composer replied:

'Oh, they are ever so useful in the daytime, and at night I can take them out and use them as a rosary.'

Such jests sat uneasily with the composer's former religious faith. The perceptive music critic Ernest Newman, who knew Elgar well, thought his Catholicism existed only insofar as it was bound up with the artistic impulse:

> Like all highly-strung human beings, he was a mass of seeming contradictions. This was nowhere more evident to me than in his views on religion. As everyone knows, he was a devout Catholic. But I often discussed philosophical – *not* religious – questions with him, and I can vouch for it that on these he invariably turned a purely philosophic mind. Where all matters of this kind were concerned he was a dual being, coolly rational when the matter under discussion was purely intellectual, religious when it was artistic in the first and intellectual only in the second place. His Catholicism seemed to me to be in large part the product of the impact on him from boyhood onwards of all the magnificent art that Christian emotion has called into being throughout so many centuries. And so, when put to a sharply realistic test his religion, I think, was apt to give him scant support.

*

Sometimes Elgar's ideas as expressed in private conversations with friends led to public statements of a remarkable and perhaps deliberately provoking nature, for example in an exchange of letters with a certain Canon Lacey of Worcester Cathedral which took place over three consecutive issues of the *Worcester Daily Times* in March, 1926. The Canon had heard that an excerpt from Wagner's *Parsifal* was to be played at that year's Three Choirs Festival and considered that Wagner's sensuality, especially in the context of his quasi-religious final work, was incompatible with Cathedral performance:

> Sir, – In the "Times Literary Supplement" of February 18th, a leading article on Beethoven contained the following remarks about Wagner : – "His emotions and spiritual experiences were those of the ordinary sensual man. From the delirium of sensual love to that craving for the refreshing ministrations of white-robed angels that follows exhaustion by fever, he expressed the whole spiritual progress from youthful pride of life to rapt and holy contemplation as it is understood by the sensualist."

A year and a half ago Mr. Paul Scippel of Zurich, after attending a performance of "Parsifal" at Bayreuth, wrote in the same sense, but more severely, in the "Journal de Genève."

I understand that an excerpt from "Parsifal" is to be included in the programme of the Musical Festival at Worcester Cathedral next September. – Your obedient servant.

T. A. Lacey

In the event, it was the Prelude to Act 1 of *Parsifal* that was played in the Cathedral. It had been heard at six previous Festivals, dating back to that at Hereford 1891, and excerpts from Acts 1 and 3 had been given on no fewer than nine occasions, beginning in 1897, again at Hereford. Both ventures were no doubt owing to the enterprise of George Robertson Sinclair, the Hereford organist and friend of Elgar. The composer was stung into an immediate, Draconian response:

Sir, – A letter in your issue of March 15 is so strange, considering the position of the writer, that a comment may be allowed and even welcome. To the depths of pruriency to which modern criticism descends I do not propose to accompany Canon Lacey; much as he seems to enjoy such exploration – I do not. The doctrine of repentance and forgiveness does not seem to be within the Canon's vision. It has been held by writers other than those quoted by Canon Lacey that Wagner's last work was an offering on the altar of sorrow and repentance. On this view I offer no opinion, but if the Canon bans Wagner from the services of the Church, he must, if he is logical, cast out David and others. As to the "delirium of sensual love and that craving for the refreshing ministrations of white-robed angels," has the Canon forgotten John Donne who, after experiencing the same travail, ended his life as a Dean in the same Church of England of which Canon Lacey is such a distinguished, if a somewhat disingenuous, ornament.

The Canon quotes "His emotions and spiritual experiences were those of the ordinary sensual man." But "Aren't we all?" If the Canon really believes that such emotions in early life debar a man from taking part in the services of the church in riper years he should at once resign his canonry and any other spiritual offices he is paid to hold. – Yours faithfully,

Edward Elgar

The letter amounted to a strange mixture of humane common-sense, sarcasm and deliberate insult. While Elgar's purely musical views would have commanded respect, his outspoken personal attack on the Canon must have been the cause of many raised eyebrows in Worcester. Whatever the rights and wrongs of the argument, the episode says a great deal about Elgar's lack of respect for the

Church establishment. It may not be without significance, too, that he called on one of the great Metaphysical poets in support of his argument. But the Canon returned to the fray, briefly and with dignity, made his moral point, and the correspondence was over:

> Sir, – Sir Edward Elgar misses the point. The writers whom I quoted were not criticising Wagner's life or character, but his art, in which they found sensuality of pietism matching the sensuality of his erotics. It was this that attracted my attention, for in my work as a priest I have had acquaintance with both kinds of sensuality, and I know which kind is the more dangerous. – Your obedient servant,
> T. A. Lacey.

*

When the time came for the next Worcester Festival, that of 1929, Elgar seemed ready to seek out another confrontation with the Cathedral authorities. This time it was on his own ground, music, and it gave rise to a truly extraordinary episode. He suggested to his old friend and devoted supporter Ivor Atkins, the Worcester organist, that he would provide a new work for the Festival. Atkins, together with many others, had for a long time been trying to coax Elgar into completing his oratorio trilogy, the final part of which, *The Last Judgement*, had remained in sketch form for many years. But Elgar's proposal was for settings of two poems by the revolutionary atheist, Shelley, *The Demon* and *Adonais*. Atkins duly sounded out the Dean of Worcester, Dr. Moore Ede, and received this reply:

> It will be a great thing if Sir Edward Elgar will produce a great work for the Festival. It will be good for the Festival, good for England and good for the world to be enriched by another of Sir Edward's masterpieces. I would do any thing in my power to assist Sir Edward.
> I have looked through the two poems you mentioned – 'The Demon' and 'Adonais' – As poems they are beautiful – 'Adonais' is the best, but it is frankly pagan. I have been trying to see if it can be twisted into a Christian poem. It is not possible. The Festivals aim at the encouragement of Church music, or great works of music, Christian in character, and suitable for a Cathedral as a Christian Temple. I do not see how we can regard Shelley's poems, even if somewhat edited, as suitable for the Cathedral. Can Sir Edward not find some poem suitable? He found the right thing in Gerontius. Is there no other poem of that class which he can take as the basis of his work?

The Dean's second paragraph rather belied his first, but as Elgar subsequently wrote to Atkins: "I don't see (really) what else he *could* say but Shelley is 'off.' I fear I cannot turn on another subject so easily . . ." Although the poet's work had powerfully engaged Elgar's creativity many years before, in the part-song setting of the *Ode to the West Wind* and in the citation of the Song, *Rarely, Rarely, Comest Thou, Spirit of Delight!* as the emotional basis of the Second Symphony, no sketches for these later settings appear to survive and it is difficult to escape the feeling that Elgar could not resist an opportunity of seeing just how far he could go in embarrassing the Dean.

The poem that gentleman referred to as 'The Demon' was presumably *The Daemon of the World*, a reworking of parts of *Queen Mab*. This youthful polemical and ideological poem which Shelley had published in 1813 attacked the constitutional, religious, commercial and military establishments of the time and advocated a brave new world of republicanism, free love and atheism. If one is tempted to feel how much the opening lines of *The Daemon* might have appealed to Elgar –

> How wonderful is Death,
> Death and his brother Sleep!
> One pale as younder wan and hornèd moon,
> With lips of lurid blue,
> The other glowing like the vital morn,
> When throned on ocean's wave
> It breathes over the world:
> Yet both so passing strange and wonderful!

- one wonders what new challenge he would have found in

> Awhile the Spirit paused in ecstasy.
> Yet soon she saw, as the vast spheres swept by,
> Strange things within their belted orbs appear.
> Like animated frenzies, dimly moved
> Shadows, and skeletons, and fiendly shapes,
> Thronging round human graves, and o'er the dead
> Sculpturing records for each memory
> In verse, such as malignant gods pronounce,
> Blasting the hopes of men, when heaven and hell
> Confounded burst in ruin o'er the world:
> And they did build vast trophies, instruments
> Of murder, human bones, barbaric gold,
> Skins torn from living men, and towers of skulls
> With sightless holes gazing on blinder heaven,
> Mitres, and crowns, and brazen chariots stained
> With blood, and scrolls of mystic wickedness,

The sanguine codes of venerable crime.
The likeness of a thronéd king came by,
When these had passed, bearing upon his brow
A threefold crown; his countenance was calm,
His eye severe and cold; but his right hand
Was charged with bloody coin, and he did gnaw
By fits, with secret smiles, a human heart
Concealed beneath his robe; and motley shapes,
A multitudinous throng, around him knelt,
With bosoms bare, and bowed heads, and false looks
Of true submission, as the sphere rolled by.
Brooking no eye to witness their foul shame,
Which human hearts must feel, while human tongues
Tremble to speak, they did rage horribly,
Breathing in self-contempt fierce blasphemies
Against the Daemon of the World, and high
Hurling their armèd hands where the pure Spirit,
Serene and inaccessibly secure,
Stood on an isolated pinnacle,
The flood of ages combating below,
The depth of the unbounded universe
 Above, and all around
Necessity's unchanging harmony.

Adonais, Shelley's great elegy on the death of John Keats, was, as the Dean said, the better poem. But its philosophy was a whole world away from that of Newman's *The Dream of Gerontius*.

Peace, peace! he is not dead, he doth not sleep –
He hath awakened from the dream of life –
'Tis we, who lost in stormy visions, keep
With phantoms an unprofitable strife,
And in mad trance, strike with our spirit's knife
Invulnerable nothings. – *We* decay
Like corpses in a charnel; fear and grief
Convulse us and consume us day by day,
And cold hopes swarm like worms within our living clay.

He lives, he wakes – 'tis Death is dead, not he;
Mourn not for Adonais. – Thou young Dawn,
Turn all thy dew to splendour, for from thee
The spirit thou lamentest is not gone;

8

Ye caverns and ye forests, cease to moan!
Cease, ye faint flowers and fountains, and thou Air,
Which like a mourning veil they scarf hadst thrown
O'er the abandoned Earth, now leave it bare
Even to the joyous stars which smile on its despair!

*

If Elgar's religious faith had been uncertain for many years, it might seem at this time not only to have disappeared, but to have turned against itself. His friend the staunch Catholic Mary Anderson de Navarro wrote to a clerical acquaintance shortly after the composer's death in 1934: 'I would rather not have my name connected with any thing concerning his faith, about two years ago I pulled him up soundly on saying he was making a new religion by taking all the '*nots*' from the Commandments & putting them into the Creed, but that was when he was very intimate with Shaw.'

Elgar's relationship with Bernard Shaw, although perhaps more ambivalent than is usually recognised, was certainly another significant factor in the composer's life and thought during the twenties and in the inception of the Third Symphony. As a young and brilliant London music critic during the 1870s, '80s and '90s, Shaw had felt the lack of a major English composer and had looked forward to 'the advent of a genius big enough and strong enough to set himself against us all and cram his ideas down our throats, whether we like them or not.' But the earliest documentary evidence of his opinion of Elgar's music appears to show no genuine instinctive recognition of it. An acquaintance remembered:

> . . . I again met Shaw at the Olivier's house, where the daughters and some young friends gave a creditable performance of The Admirable Bashville, which Shaw came down to see . . . before dinner I played one of Elgar's Enigma variations – the Nimrod variation, a noble sound portrait of Elgar's friend, A. J. Jaeger. When the last chord had been played, Shaw came into the room and asked what the piece was. I told him, and he said he had been listening to it as he was coming downstairs and could find nothing distinguished or original in it. He added: 'I know very little of Elgar's music, but I suppose that with his high reputation he must be a good composer.'

Later, and with the benefit of hindsight, Shaw would provide another version of his reaction to the Variations, writing that he had '. . . expected nothing from any English composer . . . But when I heard the Variations . . . I sat up and said "Whew!" I knew we had got it at last.' When Elgar fully emerged as a great composer during the early 1900s, GBS had given up regular music criticism and was devoting himself to his career as a playwright. The Elgars were able to spend much more time in London, and became frequent theatregoers, but Shaw's socialism and atheism were repugnant to them both at this time. A reading of *Man and Superman* was enough to convince Elgar that

> Bernard Shaw is hopelessly wrong, as all these fellows are, on fundamental things: – amongst others they punch Xtianity & try to make it fit their civilization instead of making their civilization fit it. He is an amusing liar, but not much more . . .

And a few years later he told Troyte Griffith that he thought *The Devil's Disciple*, which he saw together with Alice, 'a poor play . . the thing lacks conviction: Shaw is very *amateurish* in many ways.' It remains an opinion not entirely without currency in Shaw criticism. 'Play unconvincing,' was Alice Elgar's opinion; it was the scenery that had been the great attraction, for it had been designed by Griffith himself. Some weeks before Elgar had seen *You Never Can Tell*, but there is no record of his reaction. Alice seems to have enjoyed *The Doctor's Dilemma,* which the Elgars attended on Boxing Day, 1913, finding it 'very interesting.'

But when the two men finally met in March 1919, as part of a small luncheon party given by Lalla Vandervelde, the socialist wife of the Belgian Minister of Justice, their rapport over the common ground of music was immediate. Elgar quoted approvingly from Shaw's biting and witty music criticism and the pair dominated the conversation, somewhat to the embarrassment of their hostess. During his Birmingham lectures some fifteen years earlier, Elgar had acknowledged the seriousness of purpose which lay behind Shaw's musical writings, despite all the persiflage. Shaw had repeatedly made various specific points of which one is tempted to say Elgar would have wholeheartedly approved, about English philistinism and the nature of the musical world of the time, about the star system of singers and instrumentalists, about the stranglehold of academic and scholarly pretension, about the domination of an establishment clique, about the continuing deadly mediocrity of the festival oratorio market and about the need for municipal support for orchestral music and opera. Both men were keen in support of progress as represented by Wagner, and somewhat less enthusiastic towards Brahms, especially over his *Requiem*. Elgar preferred Verdi's and Shaw on one occasion wrote of 'the intolerable tedium of sitting unoccupied whilst the Bachists conscientiously maundered through' the work. 'Mind,' he continued, 'I do not deny that the Requiem is a solid piece of musical manufacture. You feel at once that it could only have come from the establishment of a first-class undertaker.' That was another link between composer and playwright – their capacity to generate and enjoy humour.

On the strength of that luncheon conversation Shaw was invited to Severn House for a private performance of the recently completed Piano Quintet, and his ensuing letter of critical praise further nourished the friendship. Shaw became a generous public supporter as well as a friend of Elgar, contributing an enthusiastic article about him to the first number of *Music & Letters*, and sending a classic letter of protest to the *Daily News* after a poorly attended performance of *The Apostles*: ' . . . I apologise to posterity for living in a country where the capacity and tastes of schoolboys and sporting costermongers are the measure of metropolitan culture.' If the lonely Elgar began to make a point of seeking out company among the theatrical world, Shaw became a regular attender at the Three Choirs Festivals, and the two met often at the recording studios as Elgar committed more and more of his works to disc. Shaw would later contribute to the public protest over Professor E. J. Dent's criticism of the composer, published in a German encyclopaedia, and during the Malvern Festival of 1929, made a speech praising him as one of the greatest composers in the world – if somewhat neglected by his own countrymen – and recognising the composer's art as greater than his own. Elgar replied that he knew his friend's works from beginning to end and referred to them as 'one masterpiece after another.' The composer continued by saying that Shaw knew more about music than he himself did and concluded by referring to him as 'the most amiable of men . . . the best friend a man could have . . . the kindest and possibly the dearest fellow on earth.' Elgar, whose early struggles marked him for life, particularly valued Shaw's kindness to young people embarking on their careers. He could separate the man from his work, as he told Sidney Colvin:

> GBS's politics are, to me, appalling, but he is the kindest-hearted, gentlest man I have met outside the charmed circle which includes you – to young people he is kind . . . as a child & as a young man & as a mature man, no single person was ever kind to me, so my heart goes out to any man or woman of such assured position as G. B. S. who helps others.

In the light of later developments it remains difficult to decide if the relationship amounted to anything more than a mutual admiration society, and a temporary one at that, but at the least it gave Shaw the simple satisfaction of being close to a great and admired musical figure, as it gave Elgar the opportunity to receive the reassurance that he needed, and to move more easily into the world of ideas stirring behind the retired Army officer façade. And Shaw was among the earliest to encourage the Third Symphony into being. 'Your turn now. Clap it with a symphony,' he told Elgar at the beginning of 1929, writing proudly of his new, rapidly-achieved play *The Apple Cart*.

Hesketh Pearson elicited Shaw's understanding of Elgar's religious thinking at this time, an understanding similar enough to Newman's:

11

I asked Shaw whether Elgar had been a very devout Roman Catholic.
'Good heavens, no! He avoided the subject with a deliberate reticence which convinced me that he was a nineteenth century unbeliever, though he wouldn't have admitted it and wouldn't have liked to be told so. As he was the musical hero of the three great Protestant cathedrals of Worcester, Gloucester and Hereford, and really belonged to Worcester in his soul, the world did not think of him as an R. C. All his emotion went into his music.'

Other more longstanding friends could not but be aware of some ambiguity in the relationship between Elgar and Shaw. The critic H. C. Colles wrote down a conversation with Billy Reed which took place as the pair returned by train to London after the composer's memorial service at Worcester in March 1934. Reed said:

> . . . after Lady Elgar's death he took up with a set of people who were not those of his old life at all and who made him think it was smart or up-to-date or something to be irreligious.
> Bernard Shaw, I suppose, said I.
> Exactly; he was awfully flattered because instead of lampooning him Shaw gave out that he [Elgar] was the only great composer, the only man indeed who could do anything still in music . . . It was not a real friendship. Elgar liked Shaw's brilliant talk. He took to asking me round because Shaw was going to be there and I used to go in afterwards whenever I could. I preferred that. I always knew that sort of thing was not Elgar's real self.

'It was not a real friendship . . . that sort of thing was not Elgar's real self.' Some further weight might be added to this by a reminiscence of a mutual friend, Barry Jackson, the theatre producer and director who founded the Birmingham Repertory Theatre and the Malvern Drama Festival. 'I remember GBS and Elgar once discussing inspiration,' he told an interviewer from *The Times*. 'They both agreed that they simply sat at a desk with a pencil in their hands and a piece of paper in front of them. Then something happened. It always seemed to me that there must be more to it than that.' It flatly contradicted Elgar's celebrated 'Music is in the air all around you, and you simply take as much as you want' philosophy, almost as if, in the presence of the rationalist Shaw, Elgar felt constrained to play down his romantic side. One is tempted to suspect that at the deepest level, the natures of the two men were little short of incompatible.

But on the surface the friendship was often convivial. The two men could behave like a pair of schoolboys at times, stealing apples from shops and gleefully delighting in dance tunes such as Jay Wilbur's foxtrot, 'I thought I heard a chicken sneeze, oh, Mo'nah.'

*

At length, some ten years after Alice's death, Elgar's creativity began to stir again. In 1929 he had used an Ordnance Survey map to note an idea which came to him while out driving, and the following year he was able to work it up into a fresh and masterly new *Pomp & Circumstance* March, the fifth, and one of the best of the set. It was given a rapturous reception at its Queen's Hall première under Sir Henry Wood. And after much persuasion, he agreed to provide a test piece, the *Severn Suite*, for the 1930 Crystal Palace Brass Band Competition. Although the work was built on earlier sketches and instrumented by another hand, Shaw was hugely delighted to be its dedicatee and made a point of attending its first performances at the Crystal Palace; once more, there was a generous and flattering letter to the composer. Shaw continued to take every opportunity to encourage, although other and younger musicians privately expressed reservations. Philip Heseltine, who had also attended the Crystal Palace competition in bibulous style, characteristically wrote to E. J. Moeran:

> The 'Severn Suite' is all balls, of course. We contrived . . . to spend a very amusing half-day at the Palace; the promoter of the show was very pleased with the publicity given to it by the Telegraph and caused the booze to flow freely.

But in the same letter Heseltine commented: 'My greatest musical experience has been Elgar's second symphony, of which the old gentleman gave a most moving performance.' The composer had conducted the work at the Queen's Hall a few days before, receiving a standing ovation on his appearance, and another at the end of the performance. Richard Capell of the *Daily Mail* wrote,

> It was not the first Elgar concert of the season, but it was the first time the Promenaders were able to greet the great man in person. There were scenes surpassing cordiality. The veteran composer was assisted by one of the cellists to mount to the high rostrum while the air was filled with the cheering . . . At the end of the splendid performance there was an ovation – an abused word, but it really was an ovation this time. No man on earth but must have felt touched by such tribute from assembled thousands.

In the audience was another young musician, the sixteen year-old Benjamin Britten, just beginning his period as a student at the Royal College of Music. He was at that time strongly temperamentally antipathetic to much of Elgar's music, although he would mellow in later years. But that evening of 2nd October, 1930 he was unable to sit the Symphony out, as he explained in a diary entry reflecting a full and busy day of music:

I go to College for lesson with Ireland, but he doesn't turn up (rehearsal); so I walk back to Prince's Sq. for a time, & go back at 12.0 for Mr. Allchin's class. Practise 2.0 – 4.0 in afternoon. Go (having had early dinner) to Queen's Hall & prom. – Purcell Trumpet Voluntary, Goossen's Oboe Concerto (beautiful, monotonous, impossibly gorgeously immortally played by Léon). Two V. William's songs; J. Ireland Pft Concerto (very beautiful, interestingly & excellently played). Elgar 2nd Symphony, (dreadful (nobilmente sempre) – I come out after 3rd movement – so bored. He conducts – ovation beforehand!!!!!!!!!)

The following year Elgar completed and scored the eight-movement *Nursery Suite*, again at least partially based on earlier material, but consisting of much better music than the brass band piece. The game, as Sherlock Holmes might have said, was afoot.

Indeed, 1931 proved to be a turning point. Recognition, stimulus and encouragement came thick and fast throughout the year. Professor Dent's criticism of Elgar's music was greeted by a – no doubt gratifying – storm of protest. This took the form of a letter with some nineteen signatories, including Shaw and many of the younger generation of composers, sent to the leading newspapers of England and Germany. Elgar was invited to conduct at the *Daily Express* 'Empire Celebration' at Hyde Park in May. The *Nursery Suite* was recorded in the presence of Shaw and the Duke and Duchess of York, later King George VI and Queen Elizabeth, that month, and given its first public performance at a Promenade Concert in August. Its reception was good; the *Daily Telegraph* critic in particular was able to put his finger on a new quality in the music:

The composer may call this nursery music; but those of us who have ears know well that this score . . . is the sublimation of eternal youth. There is a philosophy, a metaphysic in this music that comes from one of the subtlest intellects of our time . . . Like Verdi in his day, our Elgar appears to grow younger and more masterful as the years pass.

Basil Maine's biography of the composer, a two-volume study, was mooted, and in June Elgar was given the special recognition of a baronetcy, styling himself first Baronet of Broadheath. At the Gloucester Three Choirs Festival in September he conducted *The Dream of Gerontius,* the Violin Concerto and the *Nursery Suite* despite troublesome bouts of sciatica and nettlerash. And early in October he conducted his Second Symphony once more at a packed Queen's Hall, visibly flushing with pleasure when the whole audience again rose to greet him as he made his way to the podium.

Earlier complaints of neglect may have been forgotten by the composer as the autumn continued busy. In November the Worshipful Company of Musicians invited Elgar to a dinner in London and made him their first honorary freeman; a week later he opened the famous Abbey Road recording studios in St. John's Wood, conducting *Land of Hope and Glory* for the film cameras, and, with Shaw again in attendance, conducting the first complete recording of his Symphonic Study, *Falstaff*. The recording was mentioned during a conversation Elgar had a little time later at the Langham Hotel with a shy and admiring Eric Fenby, the young organist who had volunteered to live and work with the blind and partly paralysed Delius at his home in France in order to help him to continue composing. Fenby was en route for a Yorkshire Christmas. 'Tell Delius I grow more like Falstaff every day,' was Elgar's cheerful parting shot. And as if to cap all the honour and attention the composer was receiving, HMV made the first proposals for the wonderful young violinist Yehudi Menuhin to record the Violin Concerto with him the following year.

*

During this busy, stimulating period one engagement in particular would come to stand out as being of crucial importance despite its apparently routine nature. It was an invitation to conduct an all-Elgar concert at the third Croydon Triennial Festival, consisting of the *Meditation* from *The Light of Life*, *For the Fallen* – with Remembrance Day in mind – and *The Dream of Gerontius*, with the London Symphony Orchestra. Two other concerts, conducted by Henry Wood, were to complete the Festival, and would feature music by Franck, Delius, Grieg, Richard Strauss, Vaughan Williams, Constant Lambert, and various local composers including Elgar's close friend Billy Reed, who lived in Croydon. The town had something of a tradition of attracting musical talent, in fact, having nurtured both Samuel Coleridge-Taylor and William Hurlstone. The Festival's ambitious programme, emphasizing music by English composers, was made possible both through Reed's work as leader of the LSO and as conductor of the Croydon Symphony Orchestra, and through the zeal and ability of the founder and conductor of the Croydon Philharmonic Society, Alan Kirby, (1889 – 1959). Kirby, a dedicated amateur, had a high reputation as a chorus trainer, and he had been devoted to Elgar's music after taking part in a performance of *The Kingdom* as a teenager. In particular his ambitions became centred on giving ideal interpretations of the composer's oratorios.

For most of his life Kirby was a City stockbroker, enabling him to become conductor of both the Stock Exchange Male Voice Choir and its Operatic Society. He took over a Croydon church choir and after a highly successful *Messiah* at the South Croydon Congregational Church in 1914, was made conductor of the Croydon Sacred Harmonic Society, out of which splendidly Victorian-sounding institution the Croydon Philharmonic Society developed. Kirby conducted it for over forty years, and took it to a pinnacle of excellence. The choir became recognised as one of the best in the country and probably the finest in southern

England. Its performances of *The Apostles* and *The Kingdom*, works of which Kirby was a committed advocate despite their periods of neglect, came to be regarded as totally authoritative, even more convincing than those at Three Choirs Festivals. The Choir were invited to sing at Queen's Hall on several occasions, and in post-war years Kirby was one of the few amateurs to conduct at an Albert Hall Promenade Concert when he stood in for an indisposed Malcolm Sargent to conduct *The Music Makers*. Critical opinion was high. Ferrucio Bonavia wrote in the *Musical Times*: 'Kirby and his Philharmonic represent, for me at least, the highest point so far gained in the interpretation of Elgar's music.' And after the conductor's obituary had appeared in *The Times*, no less an Elgarian than Adrian Boult wrote to add his own thoughts:

> May I be allowed to supplement your note on the late Alan Kirby from repeated experiences of working with the Croydon Philharmonic Society? As you say, their performances of Elgar had the seal of the composer's approval, but there are many besides the composer who can agree that Alan Kirby's intense selflessness, zeal, knowledge, and understanding of the Elgar oratorios, together with his unwavering pursuit of nothing less than artistic completeness, infected every member of his choir with a "spirit of understanding" which gave their performances a quality far beyond that of an ordinary concert. He has set a standard for us all which will be indeed hard to maintain.

And during the course of another obituary in the *Musical Times,* Boult wrote of Kirby:

> To hear him direct *The Apostles* and *The Kingdom* was to gain an insight into these works and to feel a spiritual experience which comes only too rarely in the concert hall. Their message, one felt, was throughly understood by every member of the choir, so often and so completely had their magnetic conductor studied the works with them, and the resulting performances were not just concerts of rare beauty, but acts of worship of deep significance.

During his career Alan Kirby became joint founder and chairman of the National Federation of Music Societies, co-treasurer and later honorary secretary of the Royal Philharmonic Society, member of the court of the Musicians' Company, an honorary member of the Royal Academy of Music, and an honorary Fellow of Trinity College of Music. In 1950 he was awarded the O. B. E. But perhaps the honour that meant most to him was the freedom of the borough of Croydon, in recognition of his achievement in putting the town indelibly on Britain's musical map. It was a place which had a tradition of performing Elgar's music to the highest standards, and where the man himself would be welcomed as an honoured guest.

*

The Elgar concert was to take place on Tuesday, 10th November and the composer conducted the second of two rehearsals which took place at Croydon on Saturday 7th. Altogether the choir undertook five hours of preparation that day. Kirby's meticulous requirements in matters of dress were as particular as his musical standards. The first, two-hour, rehearsal took place in the parish church: '*Ladies must wear hats,* preferably small ones,' ran the rubric of the 'Information and Instuctions to Members of the Chorus.' Matters were somewhat more relaxed for Elgar's three-hour evening session, but there was no choice: 'Ladies will not wear hats,' was the instruction here.

Local pride in the Festival ran high and that day the worthy "Amphion" of the weekly *Croydon Advertiser* offered a preview.

MUSIC FESTIVAL

SOME NOTES ON NEXT WEEK'S EVENT
(BY AMPHION)

To-morrow (Sunday) the third Croydon Triennial Musical Festival will open with a dedicatory service in the Parish Church at which the Bishop of Croydon (Archdeacon E. S. Woods) will deliver an address. The Festival proper will consist of three concerts, in the Baths Hall, on Tuesday, Thursday and Saturday evenings. Some notes on the music to be heard at these three concerts, and on the artists by whom it will be performed, may be of interest . . . "The Dream of Gerontius" . . . composed over thirty years ago, is an oratorio for chorus, orchestra and three soloists . . . It remains Elgar's masterpiece in this genre. Probably most musicians would put it among the best half-dozen works of its kind in all music . . . the subject found in Elgar a composer of genius, of precisely the cast of mind and temperament for which it calls. Rarely can a literary work have found so ideal an interpreter.

Technically "The Dream of Gerontius" has some Wagnerian qualities (the leitmotif system, for example, is followed to some extent) and in the plastic quality of the music, responding at every moment to the emotional demands of the words, it is the most aesthetically satisfying of all oratorios. The first part of the work, in which are depicted the death agonies of Gerontius, is highly dramatic. The second part, treating of the experiences of the soul after it has passed over, contains some of the most serenely beautiful music ever written.

COMPOSER AS CONDUCTOR

Certain distinguished British conductors interpret Elgar's music extremely well. It is no reproach to them, however, to say that to hear "Gerontius" under Sir Edward Elgar himself is in the nature of a revelation. I will say no more on this point, but leave those who know the work to judge for themselves . . .

The Festival chorus, a hundred and sixty strong, has been at work for several months on these works. The result of their labours should gratify the musical ear next week. They have had as trainer (if he will pardon the term) Mr. A. J. Kirby, in whose fitness for the job everybody concerned, from Sir Henry Wood downwards, has complete confidence.

AT REHEARSAL

Sir Henry Wood cemented his good relations with the Festival Choir at their rehearsal on Wednesday evening. At the end he was given a great ovation. He thanked the choir for their labours and expressed his satisfaction at the standard of efficiency achieved. So everything seems to point towards the artistic success of the festival.

With the scene thus suitably set, the *Croydon Times* was able to follow up on the Monday with an account of Elgar's arrival for the rehearsal and the special arrangements made for the great man's reception.

SIR EDWARD ELGAR

GREAT RECEPTION ON ARRIVAL AT CROYDON

The Croydon Triennial Musical Festival Choir were entertained to tea at Grant's restaurant on Saturday, by the kindness of the treasurer (Alderman A. J. Camden Field), preparatory to the rehearsal of The Dream of Gerontius under Sir Edward Elgar, at the Baths Hall. The Mayor and Mayoress of Croydon were present, also Alderman H. Keatley Moore (Chairman of the Festival), Mr. W. C. Berwick Sayers (Secretary) and Mr. A. J. Kirby (Chorus Master).

As an appreciation of Mr. Kirby's work during months of preparation for the Festival, the chorus presented him with conductor's scores of Vaughan Williams's "Sea Symphony," Parry's "Blest Pair of Sirens" and Stanford's "Songs of the Sea," and a propelling pencil.

Mr. Kirby stated that his work with the chorus had been twelve months of pleasure. Their discipline had been marvellous, and it was only unfortunate that they should have broken it in that way!

A great ovation was accorded Sir Edward Elgar when he arrived with his friend, Mr. W. H. Reed, and the famous composer was briefly welcomed by the Mayor on behalf of the town.

Sir Edward replied that he was overwhelmed by the warmth of his reception. He knew Croydon largely through the fame of its Whitgift Almshouses, where he had hoped to be invited to stay the night!

After the rehearsal Sir Edward expressed his pleasure at the work of the chorus.

In the next number of the *Advertiser* "Amphion" was able to embroider the scene somewhat : –

The entire company stood up and cheered when the distinguished figure of Sir Edward Elgar, accompanied by his friend, Mr. W. H. Reed, appeared. It was a touching and spontaneous tribute to a great composer from a body which has had the best of opportunities of gaining intimate acquaintance with the beauties of one of his finest works.

Sir Edward was greeted by the Mayor and Mayoress and Alderman Keatley Moore, the vice-chairman of the Festival, and then Alderman Lewis formally welcomed him to Croydon in the name of the whole Corporation.

In a few simple sentences the composer expressed his thanks. There was no flowery language – which indeed would come oddly from one who looks very much more like a retired general than the conventional picture of a great musician – and there was a touch of humour in his reference to the famous Whitgift Almshouses, " where I hoped to be asked to stay for the night."

So Elgar the public figure, the retired general, went once more through the routines of a civic reception and made in response the public kind of speech that was expected of him, with its predictable, practised touch of local humour. That was what the public record showed. But the occasion would set the seventy-four-year-old composer's private world alight again, for it was the day, after all these years, just at the right moment, that he met the 'human spark.'

Chapter 1   The Story of November 7th, 1931

You think it horrible that lust and rage
Should dance attention upon my old age;
They were not such a plague when I was young;
What else have I to spur me into song ?

W. B. Yeats

Her name was Vera Rebecca Hockman and it seems to have been a case of love at first sight. Mrs Hockman was one of several local members of Billy Reed's Croydon orchestra accomplished enough to join the violins of the London Symphony Orchestra throughout the Festival. Gifted with an affectionate, thoughtful good nature, she was a dark-haired, dark-eyed Jewish lady in her thirties from a family with a successful business background in South African diamond mining. Vera's father, who died when she was twelve, had been one of the leading diamond merchants in England, in fact, with an international reputation extending to Antwerp and New York. The youngest of three children, Vera had been brought up in a fashionable London house at Portchester Terrace boasting liveried servants and a carriage and pair, and had been given a good private education followed by what she called a 'globe-trot' round the world. But her antecedents left her nevertheless with a strong dislike of ostentation or any suggestion of money-making for its own sake, and a spiritual rather than a specifically religious outlook. Intelligent, artistic and somewhat emotionally intense, Vera was slightly unconventional, needing to rise above everyday life; possibly something of an escapist, like Elgar himself. But she was nevertheless a stable and balanced personality, known and loved for a charismatic personal warmth, optimism, humour and charm.

Music had been an important, disciplined part of Vera's childhood, for she had been made to practise the violin for an hour each morning before leaving for school. Her mother Amy, a generous, demanding character, was an excellent pianist who enjoyed frequent concert-going along with the cultivation of the friendship of musical celebrities, and the London house became something of a *salon* in the inter-war years. The hours of practice under her mother's leadership paid off handsomely in many opportunities for Vera to participate in domestic chamber-music sessions, and for her to meet on terms of social ease, figures such as the singers Sarah Fischer and Pauline Donalda, the violinists Albert Sammons and Daisy Kennedy, and pianists such as Irene Scharrer, Myra Hess, Ethel Hobday – husband of the noted viola player and a friend of Brahms – and Benno Moiseivitch. And ultimately the violin would lead her to the musical friendship that she prized above all others.

20

Vera had married young, at nineteen, not unhappy perhaps to leave a home where she was still being sent up to bed before her elders, and full of admiration for the outstanding abilities of her much older suitor, Joseph, who held a Doctorate in Philology from Heidelberg University. They would have two children, a son, John, and a daughter, Dulcie. Joseph Hockman had become a rabbi in about 1909, developing a wide reputation, although it gradually became evident that Vera's temperament was not ideally suited to the rôle and duties of the wife of a minister of religion. Joseph gave up his position, and volunteered for service in the Great War, becoming an officer in the Royal Horse Artillery and seeing action under Allenby in the Middle East. He subsequently qualified as a barrister, although the new career served only to exacerbate the incompatibility with Vera, whose essentially artistic leanings meant that she could find little rapport with her husband's colleagues. She disliked having to entertain them, and resented too the sacrifice of the evening and weekend hours that Joseph, devoted to Vera though he was, had to spend working at home; the advantage of a comfortable private income meant perhaps that she had become somewhat insulated from day-to-day realities. Joseph took a post abroad in about 1927, as legal advisor to the King of Siam, hoping that absence might make his wife's heart grow fonder, but such was not to be the case and the separation became permanent. After his return to England, Joseph Hockman practised as a court-room lawyer for the rest of his life, although his kindly, reflective nature meant that the confrontational skills necessary for success did not always come easily to him. He continued to hope for a reconciliation with Vera, and kept her photographs. Dulcie took her mother's side, but John visited his father regularly in later years and remembered never having heard him say a word against Vera.

In the aftermath of the break-up of her marriage, Vera was sufficiently financially and emotionally secure to be looking forward to an independent new future, living with her children at the Shirley Park Hotel while having a house, Robin Hill, built at Pine Coombe nearby. Having developed into a capable violinist, she was a well-known, active amateur player in the London area, remembered as rushing – sometimes quite literally running – to rehearsals and concerts, violin case in hand. She was a friend of Billy Reed, and enjoyed too, like many other attractive younger women, an affectionate 'Uncle Ralph' relationship with Vaughan Williams, to whom in a regular friendship ritual she would send a calendar every year. Every year without fail there would be a letter of thanks in return. Vera played in the Leith Hill Festivals at Dorking and seems to have meet and corresponded regularly with the composer. And as second violin with a string quartet led by her friend Hazel Inglis, she took part in the first performance of his *Three Mystical Songs* for baritone, string quartet and piano, in Croydon in December 1922.

Vera was one of those whose intensity of feeling and experience created a need to make a personal record of particularly important events. As we shall see, she wrote accounts of her meetings with the two most important men in her life, and in a somewhat different if highly appropriate style she narrated her childrens' early days in home-made journals which included day-by-day doings, family photographs and tiny songs. The journals were also for her absent soldier husband's benefit. Written as if by the child herself, Dulcie's Journal reflects a strong parental bond, and, along with the occasional baby-language, much maternal sophistication and humour. On 9th November, 1920, for example, Dulcie had become exactly eight months old; the day was marked by a song, *You Beautiful Bird*, given a four-bar two-part setting in Ab major.

'You beautiful bird, you glorioush ting,
Ting ting ting ting
Ting ting ting ting.'

8 months old, I weigh 18lbs I have 3 teeth. The lord mayor's show is shorn of all its glory I am told but never mind.

Step by step, Dulcie marked her early progress through life.

10th November. I have 4 teeth & I have meat juice in my bottle. I laugh all day; my gums are better.

14th November. A big boy called Paddy comes & plays in our nursery – I heartily approve.

15th November. Behave remarkably well all day, but scandalize Mummie & Daddy by insisting upon having a hearty meal at midnight.

17th November. Florrie saves my life. On hearing me emit a distressed cry she left her work and rushed to me (Mamie & Mummie being out) and found the bell from the rattle at the back of my throat. She hurriedly fished it up with her little finger whereupon I chuckled gratefully. At the next Investiture she will receive a medal from King George – perhaps !

18th November. Auntie Doris tells stirring tales of the beauty & intelligence of Irene Scharrer's daughter, Rachel, who is a few days older than I. Poor Mummie tries in vain to make me say Mum Mum & ta to order.

19th November. My cousin arrives but I am not quite in my best form.

24th November. I now say "a-ta" starting pianissimo ending fortissimo. I love the cuckoo in the clock & watch for him to appear.

27th November. My Godmother arrives alas with a bad finger so she cannot carry me about as she used to. She rejects the current opinion that I am brainless.

1st December. Mummie sits in my pen with me and lets me push along the pretty coloured balls and at times spin them round.

3rd December. Mummie overjoyed because I called Mum-mum-mum . . .

5th December. A peaceful Sunday after a quarrel with Mrs Morgan who tried to take my Mummie's place in giving me my bottle. Initiated a short-lived Hunger Strike.

7th December. Christmas presents begin to arrive for me. I begin to know my hands are for toys and my mouth is not. But I still find my mouth useful in play – ppf . . . is an amusing sound.

8th December. Last night I ppf . . . d quite a lot and was severely rebuked by Mummie who had to give up some sleep and nurse me before I forgave her. Today, as I could not see my brother at play from my cot, I was strapped into a chair to enjoy the view.

It sounds like an idyllic infancy, bathed in mother love and the attention and support of family and friends, support which enabled Vera to go on with her music. One day two years later, with the Vaughan Williams première approaching, Dulcie went to a birthday party while her mother attended a rehearsal.

I went out to tea alone with Roguey to Robbie's birthday tea. I behaved well apart from making love to "Bert" and the thailor boys in the magic lantern picture. When Kate arrived to fetch me I was all ready & waiting just beginning to ask for Mamie. Dear Mummie came & played every sort of imaginary game. She helped me write to Father Xmas and ask for a Mrs Strang bookie & a doll drethed like a thailor boy.

The use of a private language between mother and daughter persisted to some degree into Dulcie's adulthood, almost as Edward and Alice Elgar used baby language with each other throughout their married life.

*

Music was Vera's immediate point of contact with Elgar, for whom she had already developed a feeling nothing short of hero-worship. But she possessed as well a variety of other interests, including a flair for languages and, like Elgar himself, a deep love and knowledge of literature and the natural world and a strong idealistic vein; indeed she deliberately sought at times to project a somewhat unworldly persona. When in later years the time came for her to sell Robin Hill, she was mock- scandalised to find that its value had appreciated. 'But its second-hand !' she protested. 'I've used it !' It was a splendid large house and garden in a beautiful setting amid pine trees adjacent to the Addington golf course. Knowing Vera's love and knowlegeable interest in bird-song, 'Uncle Ralph' on one occasion teasingly referred to it as her 'robin's nest.'

There can be no doubt that for both partners, her relationship with Elgar was one of the great love affairs, though doomed from the beginning by the burden of the composer's years, by the forces of convention which he had tried to shrug off as never before, and by the impossibility of Vera's marital situation. There seems every possibility that Elgar came to want to marry her, and his daughter was known to have viewed such a possibility with dismay. But without dwelling on 'what might have been,' and what cannot be known, it is very clear that Elgar enjoyed with Vera the last of a series of the romantic-inspirational relationships which may be said to have characterised his whole creative life and which generated the renewed creative impetus which led him to grapple with the Third Symphony, the Piano Concerto and *The Spanish Lady*. For that, and for the happiness that Vera brought to his last years, let us be grateful. Elgar himself was, and showed it in a tender, romantic musical vignette, one of the many feminine portraits in his music. It is to be found as the second subject of the first movement of the Third Symphony, clearly marked in the sketches as 'V. H.'s own theme.' The music is part of the minimal amount of perfectly original material in his sketches for the work.

Almost everything we know about Elgar and Vera is contained in an account, fully published herein for the first time, which she herself subsequently wrote for a small circle of close friends and which she called, 'The Story of November 7th, 1931.' Their first meeting was miraculous to them both and its date became permanently fixed in their minds, part of the private mythology of their relationship. Vera's document was written in longhand on Elgar's favourite blue Florentine notepaper, and has every sign of having been produced in a characteristically intense flow of emotion, with somewhat erratic punctuation. The result is an unconventional yet totally convincing mixture of narrative, reminiscence, conscious and unconscious humour, scripted dialogue and poetry.

It is on any terms a wonderful human document, a classic account of a love-affair from boy-meets-girl instant attraction through the first hesitant conversations and the discovery of shared interests, to the use of special names, the giving of gifts and the need to share the loved one with family and friends, thus making to some extent a public statement about the relationship. Vera paints an authentic self-portrait of a woman in love, beginning with confessions of vulnerability and self-doubt – the feelings of 'I can't believe this is happening to me' – and leading to glorious certainty, the knowledge that 'It had to happen, it was meant to happen.'

Her account veers between the straightforward and prosaic, the touchingly sentimental and naive, and the poetic and sublime. To outsiders the behaviour of two people in love can seem to border on the ridiculous at times, but Vera gradually draws us right inside the timeless, universal experience she is describing so that we share it and are part of it. She reminds us too, most importantly in the context of her story, that age is but a disguise, and that our need for love and romance does not diminish as we grow older. Elgar himself we might have expected to continue a Romantic to the end; Vera reminds us that it is natural and dignified for the elderly to fall in love.

Vera's portrait of Elgar rings true time and time again. We recognise the man we know, at ease in the house and garden at Marl Bank, his atmospheric Worcester home, with its views of the the Cathedral and the Malvern Hills beyond. We hear again of his rapport with his beloved dogs, of his wide knowledge of literature, his love of light music and his irreverent views of some of the established repertoire works. We see his quiet pride in his life's achievement, his humour, and his familiar mixture of nervousness and exuberance.

But Vera adds something to our knowledge of the composer as well, for she shows us vividly, as perhaps no-one else quite has, the volcanic nature of Elgar's temperament, the extent to which his continuing capacity for overwhelming states of feeling could erupt into uncontrollable physical restlessness and agitation. We hear such moods in his music, and indeed they must be close to the roots of his creativity, but Vera shows us this aspect of the man himself with her own unique clarity and honesty. And she was able to calm him, and offer comfort and reassurance, just as Alice had, and his mother Ann Elgar before that; Earth-Mother as well as White Goddess.

The Story of November 7th, 1931 offers other interesting sidelights, but first and foremost it is a perceptive, revealing account of a great composer, a man whom she came to understand and describe as few have done. Perhaps indeed Vera gives us the best existing single-sentence summation of the essential duality of Elgar's nature when she writes of him as 'one moment so disillusioned, materialistic, the next so mystical and visionary.'

Vera's 'story' begins with a description of her feelings in anticipation of Elgar's coming to Croydon. Like Vaughan Williams, she had been at the Queen's Hall Second Symphony performance – characteristically forgetting her violin afterwards – and had noted the signs of the poor health Elgar had been suffering; in fact the composer sat to conduct at Croydon. She continues with her own version of his official reception at Grant's and the atmosphere at the ensuing rehearsal – 'You could feel the love and veneration like great clouds of incense enveloping him.' Then, after repeated eye contact, Elgar asked to be introduced to her.

The Story of November 7th, 1931.

(Written on EE's Italian (Florentine) note paper)

In the autumn of 1931 there was to take place at the Croydon Triennial Festival a performance of *Gerontius* conducted by E. E. himself, and I was to be playing at the second desk of first violins.

My <u>one</u> (positive) thought was: I must know every note in order to give my whole attention, body and soul, to Him. My <u>other</u> (negative) thought was one of mortal fear lest he should be prevented from coming by some dreaded illness or calamity. And, indeed, he had looked very white-haired & frail & bent at the Promenade Concert only a month before at which he had conducted his glorious 2nd Symphony to my delirious joy & rapture.

I remember I had been so transported by that divine work that afterwards I walked off without my fiddle and suddenly remembering it at Oxford Circus, dashed frantically back, collided with dear V. W. at a street corner, said breathlessly,

"Wasn't the Symphony heavenly ?" and he with a huge score of it under his arm replied,

"Yes, wonderful."

"So wonderful that I have left my fiddle behind at the Hall."

"Good Heavens !" exclaimed 'Uncle Ralph' in alarmed tones.

Only a month later with that high music ringing in my ears I was to play for Him !

On November 7th the day of the rehearsal, three days before the beginning of the Croydon Festival, there was to be a huge gathering – a tea party – given at Grants, at which the Mayor of Croydon was to be present to give an official welcome to the great man to which all members of the choir and orchestra were invited.

I arrived late, having already taken part in a performance of the Brahms *Requiem* at St. Martins-in-the-Fields, and found a seat among friends at the very farthest away corner of the large tea rooms.

How often we have laughed about that occasion since for it appears that on finding himself piloted by W.H.Reed, in the Ladies' Underwear Department he began protesting violently.

"Billie, I will NOT go any further."

"Come along come along, it will be all right upstairs" said Billie reassuringly, coaxing him onwards. When he arrived – again looking very snow-white and rather bowed – we all pressed forward to catch a glimpse of him, in vain trying to hear him speak.

The Mayor stammeringly (but proudly) welcomed "Sir Edgar Ellwood" to Croydon. <u>His</u> reply was inaudible from where I stood but there were frequent bursts of merriment and I did just catch him murmuring with a twinkle in his eye something about being detained at the Whitgift Almshouses.

Then all adjourned to the rehearsal at the Baths Hall (where E. E. had no intention nor premonition whatever of going off the deep end).

The orchestra consisted of experienced Croydon players together with members of the L.S.O. Billie Reed leading, with Hazel Inglis, the leader of the Croydon Orchestra, beside him; at the second desk immediately behind was Wynn Reeves with me sitting beside him.

No sooner were we all assembled than He came. My heart stood still. It seemed as if one's whole life had been leading up to that moment. It is impossible to describe the noble dignity with which he took up his baton announcing in his quiet yet vibrant low tones – no one who had heard his voice can ever forget that distinct & distinguished enunciation – that we would begin with the *Meditation* from *The Light of Life*. And now the whole rehearsal fades into one stupendous experience which might have lasted for an hour or for an eternity. From that moment I hardly seemed to have to look at the music, my heart & soul went out to him because his way was not to command the orchestra but to implore of them to give all the fire and energy and poetry that was in them. You could feel the love and veneration like great clouds of incense enveloping him.

Then somehow he became aware that there was one whose only desire was to play as he would have it played. I distinctly remember catching his eye, small and bright with the serene expression of a God who looks upon his creation and finds it good. The first time this happened it might have been accidental, but as the rehearsal went on it occurred again and again until it became a part of that sublime dream through which I was living that whenever the first violins had to play a passionate or appealing or "molto resoluto" passage he would look at me beseechingly and yet with such an expression of happy confidence in his eyes as if to say,

"I know you understand and will do it for me."

It was a smile which can rarely be seen on this earth – perhaps it is to be seen on the faces of the choir of Angelicals who sing Praise to the Holiest in the Heights !

Gerontius over – and I remember in the melting theme of the *Angel's Farewell* he said imploringly,

"I should like to hear a still more beautiful tone from the Strings, please"

& then we played it again much more tenderly – he left the orchestra in his dignified manner having thanked the choir for their beautiful singing – "nobilmente" always.

A few minutes later I was talking to a small group of players – raving about Him – when someone touched me on the arm saying,

"Sir Edward Elgar has asked to be introduced to you."

"Good God, you're joking !" I gasped, then followed her with trembling limbs to where E. E. was standing in the hall talking to Billie Reed.

"Sir Edward has asked for you," said W. H. R.

"I noticed your playing and wanted to be introduced to you," said He.

"Oh, but this is the most wonderful experience of my life to play for you."

"I could see by your face that you understand my music," he said in that same quiet but distinct way, the words rather detached – (I can hear him now, and I always shall).

"I hope I do," was all I said, hopelessly intoxicated, (& blind to the world) for the rest of the evening.

The next day, Sunday 8th November, saw the official opening of the Festival at a dedicatory Service, preceded by an organ recital, held before a large congregation in the Croydon Parish Church. The Festival Choir took part, ('Ladies will wear white dresses, but not sleeveless dresses, and veils . . . No coloured ornaments to be worn. Gentlemen will wear dark morning dress.') singing various anthems, and giving, according to the Croydon Times *a 'beautifully rendered' performance of Coleridge-Taylor's Magnificat and Nunc Dimittis in F. Fitting the occasion, the Bishop of Croydon, Archdeacon E. S. Woods, gave an address in which he meditated on the relationship between art – especially music – and religion. With some knowledge of Elgar's turning away from religious thinking and his expressed wish to make Worcester Cathedral resound to the pagan ideas of Shelley, the worthy Bishop's thoughts, not at times altogether different from those of Canon Lacey, offer some interesting resonances.*

Commenting on the appropriateness of such a service, the Bishop said it would be a mistake to take for granted the connection between religion and music. We in this country had for many centuries shown ourselves to be both religious and musical but it had taken a long time to work out the true relationship between our religion and our music . . .

"Why," asked the Bishop, "do we feel this dedicatory service to be so eminently fitting ? Why is it that this kind of music will stir in us – and most of us, I suppose, are musically sensitive – elevated thoughts, thoughts that are good to think, thoughts that unquestionably tend to make us better men and women ? Why, on the other hand, in some regions of art today, including music, does there appear to be a complete divorce between the artist and religion?"

". . . It does seem to me," Bishop Woods went on, "a grave loss for all concerned when art is divorced from religion. That there is such a gulf between the two, and that so far attempts to bridge it have only been partially successful, is I fear undeniable. I am not thinking of art that is bad or debased. Indeed, I do not think the Kingdom of God has any room for bad art. I cannot see that any ultimate values are served by painting or sculpture that is freakish or untrue or which merely represents the cult of the ugly and decadent which is so much in the world today, or by poetry that is flabby and futile, or by music that is trivial, sentimental, or sensuous."

"But what does matter is when men who take their art seriously and are really trying to say something worth saying through their music, or their painting, seem to ignore or leave out of account the whole vast field of human aspiration and human experience which may properly be called religion."

There were many causes tending to produce that division. The slogan of "Art for Art's sake" seemed to betray the departmental mind which failed to perceive the inevitable affinities between the aesthetic, the moral and the intellectual elements in human experience. It has also to be confessed that part of the cause of the alienation was to be found in the attitude towards art and artistic things which had often characterised the Church for long periods in its history. It would be too much to claim, said the Bishop, that the Church had altogether outgrown that kind of outlook.

"There are still too many relics in our midst of the bad kind of Puritanism which was actually sour towards human joy, and which regarded all beauty as belonging to the realm of the devil."

There is no record of Elgar having attended the dedicatory service. His thoughts, like Vera's, were presumably elsewhere. They met again at the Gerontius *rehearsal and performance on Tuesday 10th November, and at the subsequent party at the Reeds', to which Elgar seems to have made sure that Vera was invited. He demanded her full attention that evening, and his conversation rapidly became personal and reminiscent. He asked about the house she was having built and made it clear that he must see her again. Emotionally drained after the music, and expecting anti-climax, the shy musician could hardly believe what was happening. But she no longer saw 'the white-haired bent old gentleman,' and quickly found a poetic identity for him with intimate associations from her youth, Hyperion.*

The next rehearsal was to be on Tuesday 10th, the day of the performance. After the Saturday rehearsal Billie Reed had come & announced to me that there was to be a party at his house after the performance of *Gerontius* and he would be so pleased if I would come to meet Sir Edward

"As he seems to have taken such a fancy to you; He said 'Who is that sweet girl, Billie, is she a pupil of yours?' and I said ' No such luck!' "

From Saturday until Tuesday I scarcely ate or slept but kept living over again and again that wonderful rehearsal always asking myself was it a dream that out of all those people he noticed <u>me</u>? In dreams those things do happen and one advances to be introduced and then discovers one has only a vest – or even less – on !

On Tuesday afternoon was the rehearsal of *Gerontius* with the soloists. Saturday had been for choir & orchestra – He arrived and this time when I rose to let him pass by to get to the rostrum he greeted me with the sweetest smile as if we had always known one another – "millions of ages back."

It was necessarily a scrappy rehearsal jumping from place to place for the soloists but He knew that I understood the music and I knew that He knew. It was grand to be alive !

After the rehearsal he came up to me quite naturally and began asking me about my playing, where I usually played, why he had not met me before, whether I could come along with him to Mr. Reed's house <u>now</u>.

"I am not allowed to leave yet alas because there are other works to rehearse but I shall be coming later on," I replied.

Mrs Gill then appeared (she was another member of the first violins) to drive him to Chatsworth Rd.

"What a responsibility to drive so precious a person," I remarked.

"Oh, no, there is nothing precious about me," he retorted in that decided way in which he invariably disparaged himself (often intending that someone should contradict him !)

Various members of the L.S.O. had by this time observed him gazing in my direction rather frequently. I must reluctantly admit that they did not think it an unprecedented occurrence as he was renownedly susceptible but I do think it was the first time that anyone actually playing in the orchestra had found such favour in his sight.

"For goodness sake don't look at him too much tonight or he will lose his place," said Wynn Reeves.

The performance that night was so divine an experience for me that I can only say that the choir sang magnificently and the whole work was raised on to some celestial plane where one no longer questions or criticizes but just floats blissfully, effortlessly along like the disembodied soul in the second part of *Gerontius*.

When it was over I felt exhausted, finished. I had no courage left to go to that party to meet Sir Edward Elgar Bart. O. M. &c &c. I had met him; our souls had been so close together for hours or was it years ? I drove with friends to Chatsworth Rd cold in body & in spirit in mortal fear of anticlimax after that bliss.

Plucking up all my courage I entered the small crowded room & shook hands with dear Mr. & Mrs. Billie (my first visit to their house) who reintroduced me to Him.

He. "We know one another already; come on, I have been waiting for you all the evening. Why are you so reluctant to come forward – have you been playing wrong notes, and are you afraid to face me now?"

I shyly went up to him saying I didn't remember doing anything specially wrong but had found it most difficult to see his beat whenever the tenor (Heddle Nash) stood up, & I was quite exhausted from dodging about trying to look at him.

"But I have been looking at you all the evening. I am afraid I have not been able to take my eyes off you."

Then I tried to disappear among the guests in order not to monopolise so distinguished a guest but he followed & found me saying,

"You are not to leave me for one moment or I shall scream."

He was being offered tea (he had a great weakness for strong tea he told me, but not for strong liquor).

"Now be a good girl and tell me whether it is Indian or China tea."

I had to confess at once that I never drink tea and don't know the difference – feeling such an ass that I couldn't carry out this his first request.

Then in spite of the numerous people wanting to shake hands with the great man we began finding out all about one another.

"We each have a black & white cocker spaniel and mine is the nicest in the world except yours," said he and began telling anecdotes about his noble Marco (who even follows him to the bathroom & lies on his dressing gown). He asked me whether I had heard *Gerontius* before.

"Good heavens I have known it all my life & know & worship every note."

"Isn't it wonderful that you should know my music ?"

Then he began singing *Sanctus Fortis*.

"That's not such a bad tune is it – are you aware that I never had a lesson in composition ?"

He spoke of the different conceptions of Gerontius & said John Coates's had been the best; he did not agree with Elwes's saintly interpretation as Gerontius was typically a man of the world in the very midst of life who dreamed this fearful dream!

"But fancy you knowing my music," he said again.

"I have always known it and loved it but never expected to know you," I said.

He asked where I lived. I told him at a hotel in Shirley while my house was being built near there in a pine wood.

HE: "Oh do you think I shall live to see it finished ?"

I: "I should think you will seeing that I am to move in next Spring."

HE: "Then will you take me to see it ? And meanwhile would you come to London and see me when next I come, because I am afraid I must see you again."

I: "I hardly know what to answer. I can't believe that you are really saying these things to me."

Then he went on to tell me about the struggles of his early days in a lawyer's office & how he had to forsake that for music. Of the numbers of violin lessons he gave for next to nothing in order that he might have his precious lessons in London with dear old Pollitzer who at once recognized him as a most gifted pupil ("but I knew I could never be a great violinist – my fingers were too thin.") By this time the white haired bent old gentleman had vanished for ever.

Now and henceforth he was Hyperion ever glorious (or sometimes My Wondrous Being).

After the party Elgar returned to his base at the Langham Hotel, from where next day the Gramophone Company car took him to the new Abbey Road Studios in St. John's Wood. In the afternoon he recorded part of his Falstaff *and next morning he returned for the official inauguration of the famous studios, completing the historic recording and conducting* Land of Hope and Glory *for the Pathé newsreel cameras. That day he returned to Worcester. But before setting off for the first* Falstaff *session he wrote to Vera, and she received the letter the same day. It was the first of a series of letters keeping the Croydon experience alive and holding out the possibility of further meetings.*

The first letter received on November 11th : – (Billie having given him my address.)

Dear Mrs. Hockman

I have to return home tomorrow; <u>please</u> tell me if we can meet next time I am here.

I really enjoyed last night although my eyes were for things other than the score, I fear.

Yrs Sincerely,
Edward Elgar.

Then a day or two after in the orchestra Billie Reed sent me his love and asked that I should write & tell him further news of the festival. In this his reply to my letter he enclosed a p. p. c. photograph which I always keep beside me ("In remembrance Croydon Festival.")

And he would send her too an autographed miniature score of his String Quartet, dated November 7th.

Dear Mrs. Hockman,

I am so much obliged to you for writing; I had a <u>most</u> pleasant time at Croydon Festival and am glad to hear anything about it. I wish you would cause the paper with the picture in it to be sent to me; I hope some of – or one of – the first violins is in it too.

I shall not be in London till December & I hope there will not be too many concerts &c.

With kind regards and again thanks,

Believe me to be,

Yrs Sincerely,

Edward Elgar.

P. S. Mr. Reed seems to have delivered the message correctly (i.e. his love)

The following Sunday, 15th November, Elgar's godson Wulstan Atkins went to see him at Marl Bank, one of many such visits that he was to make at this period which enabled him to become increasingly observant of the composer's moods. On this occasion, Atkins found him exuberant, full of 'almost boyish delight.'

In fact Elgar returned to London somewhat earlier than he had planned, for arrangements were made for him to view the Abbey Road film at the Pathé Theatre in Wardour Street. He was established at the Langham again on 25th November, and next morning took Vera by surprise by telephoning with a proposal that they meet for lunch. She was already engaged but there was no question but that she would cancel and accept Elgar's invitation. Once more she was anxious, but as soon as conversation was under way their previous rapport flourished again, and Elgar asked to see her the next day as well. They talked a good deal of poetry and nature, and shared much music together. Elgar made plain his intense need for her, and Vera began to feel that she could be entirely herself and at ease in his company. The meetings marked a special new depth in the relationship. Vera offered to visit him at Worcester, however briefly. Both knew how little time there might be.

Ten days later I was practising in my room at Shirley Park Hotel when I was called to the phone which was in the public corridor.

"Sir Edward Elgar wishes to speak to you," said the hall porter.

I nearly collapsed. Apart from anything else it was so public just there and yet I could not keep Him waiting while I descended to the box on the ground floor.

His voice was quiet but distinct and deliberate as ever:

"Speak slowly & distinctly or I shall not hear," he said, "and don't shout ! Will you come & lunch with me at the Langham Hotel today at 12. 30 ?"

"Yes – no – well that is to say I ought to be doing something else but I WILL."

"Very well then, I shall expect you at 12. 30 – thank you."

It was already past eleven. I had only time to put off the other engagement, (owing to a Royal Command) change my clothes and <u>go</u>.

I was absolutely ill with apprehension for fear I should disappoint him. It was all very well that night at Mrs. Reed's after the excitement of the performance, but at mid day in cold blood <u>in November</u> ! I cannot remember the train journey or the taxi journey. I wore a simple coat frock of reddish woolly material with gilt buttons (which he noticed almost immediately by asking whether they were bought with the frock or separately!!)

He was waiting in the big vestibule wandering hither & thither, sending off telegrams (to do with betting, I fear) writing notes, coming backwards & forwards in his restless way (no vestige of the old gentleman now). When I came he breathed one big sigh of relief.

HE: "You've come – how wonderful ! Now I can rest and be happy. How good of you to come to see such an old man."

I: "<u>Please</u> do not speak like that, it is the most overwhelming joy for me to come to you, only I can't express it in words."

HE: "Let us sit here for a little while and let me look at you and make sure it is not a dream. What lovely eyes you have . . . Oh dear I have had such a tiring morning and have been hearing so many sad things. We are together, we shall not think of any more sad things – shall we ?"

I: "No, you must just be happy and rest with me."

HE: "Will you drink a cocktail ? Waiter, bring two Manhattans please !"

(I was amazed to hear him ordering such new-fangled Yankee drinks !)Then we drank together and he gazed at me & said,

"Aren't we <u>clever</u> to have found one another. Of course I have dreamt of you all my life and knew you at once at Croydon – was it very impertinent of me to ask to be introduced ? Fancy, I have conducted a <u>million</u> times but I have never asked to be introduced to any lady in the orchestra ! Do you know that I was so afraid after the performance on 10th that I shouldn't see you again that I refused to get into the car that was waiting at the hall to take me to Billy Reed's although it was cold & I was hot. 'I am not going in till I have said goodbye to <u>her</u>, Billie.' 'Go on, get in she's coming round to my house,' said Billy, bundling me in."

"Now we must be practical & think of food. What would you like?"

"I must confess at once," I said, "that I don't notice food when I'm happy like this so please just order what you would have if I weren't here & don't let us discuss it."

HE: "Very well then I will go and order it while you sit here & wait for me, but oh <u>please</u> do not vanish while I am gone. I am so afraid I shall come back & find it is all a dream."

During those few moments I waited for him to return I was almost in tears, so overwhelmed by his humility. To think that just because he wore that disguise of old age – and how swiftly that youthful & exuberant soul broke through the disguise – he should have to feel humble before an inferior being forty years his junior ! The whole principle seemed so wrong, and how unthinkable that someone might take advantage. . oh dear me – ?

When he came back we began to speak about English poetry. His knowledge of English Literature was stupendous. He never forgot anything he had read & loved.

"I can't help it, I can't forget anything I'm interested in & can't remember anything I'm not (interested in.) For instance I've never yet learnt what was The Pragmatic Sanction."

I had read enough to know what he was talking about – he could tell that I genuinely love poetry & nature. I told him about my love of birds, and how I collect bird songs in my head, always searching for new ones. Again it might have been three hours or it might have been a life time that we were together. He would gaze & gaze into my eyes and murmur:

"Millions & millions of years, I can read it all there. Aren't you divine ? What music I would write if I could have you near to me always."

So soon it was 3. 30 & time for his next appointment and he said,

"It has been such a happy time. Will you come again tomorrow before I go back to Worcester ? The time is so short. I must see you as much as possible. I have not much longer to live."

Next morning I received a letter from the Langham written in the now familiar bold scrawly inimitable writing.

It just said : -

Thank you

Thursday evening.

By this I knew how wonderful it had been for him too. Next day when I went to him all nervousness had vanished because I knew henceforth and for ever more that we somehow miraculously understood one other; that I could be myself and perfectly at ease with him. We had so much in common, not only my love & knowledge of his own works but of all that is beautiful in music. We would sing tunes together & we both had an extraordinary memory for themes innumerable, and he would become nearly frantic with excitement ("What a man !") speaking of Wagner or Beethoven or Schumann &c. And because all my life I had worshipped him through his music and because his whole personality was in his music I was already familiar with all the moods. I knew him. Nothing seemed strange or unexpected or unfamiliar. Of course there were quaint twists and turns to his fantastic mind which no one could foresee. One moment so disillusioned & materialistic, the next moment so mystical & visionary.

Having discussed poetry together on the Thursday I took my *Pageant of English Poetry*, which I always have (& had) beside me, and together we read

35

favourite poems. I remember the first thing he quoted to me was from *Alexander's Feast* (Dryden). He threw back his head and declaimed "The princes applaud with a **FURIOUS JOY**" and "The many REND THE SKIES with loud applause." He was so thrilled with the grandeur of such lines as these, he got into a frenzy of excitement. He scribbled 'Vera' beside a fragment from *Festus* (P. J. Bailey) which he said is a long turgid poem in its entirety – he <u>knew everything</u> –

(Like this) Vera : Thou hast more music in thy voice
Than to the spheres is given,
And more temptations on thy lips
Than lost the angels heaven;
Thou hast more brightness in thine eyes
Than all the stars which burn,
More dazzling art thou than the throne
We fallen dared to spurn.

There seemed so much to be done together that a whole life time would not be long enough even if he were young " but I am so old you know & the time is so short."

"À propos of that," I said, "supposing you ever found yourself alone and free I would gladly come to Worcester just for one hour or two; distance is nothing to me."

"I will remember – perhaps telegraph when such a time comes."

And five days later the invitation came. On Thursday 3rd December, Vera entrained for Worcester with her violin for an afternoon of conversation, dogs and music. The Violin Sonata was rehearsed, and played to Elgar's niece, Madge Grafton. The close musical companionship brought the work to life all over again for the composer, and it is difficult to imagine that such an occasion would not have had a stimulating effect on Elgar's resurgent creativity. Vera makes his uninhibited excitement clear, and her description of the composer's behaviour at Marl Bank is one of the most vivid we have, with its reference to his 'gorgeous medley of Michaelangelesque grand faults & virtues.'

On December 2nd came the following telegram : -

"Could you come tomorrow meet train Worcester 12.43" (Reply paid Elgar Worcester). It had been waiting for me all day while I was out playing in town. Agitated at keeping him waiting for an answer I wired back "Will come." Next morning this letter from Worcester: -

Thank you for your letter which is what I wanted.
I am sending a telegram but I fear it is too late: if so next week Wednesday ?

I understand that you wish to go through the Sonata with me. I shall be glad to attempt the piano part – there is a violin here.

Ever,

E. E.

My fiddle & I went. He was waiting at the Station in the car with the two dogs: Spaniel & Cairn, Marco & Mina (male & female) with whom I made friends at once. It was only two minutes drive to Marl Bank: One moment in the ugly slummy part of Worcester the next in his dear quiet old-world house on Rainbow Hill with the lovely old lawns seeming to slope up & up to the Cathedral tower, the base line of the Malvern Hills beyond. Not a house in sight though in reality it was in the midst of them.

It was just the place for him: garden, cathedral, hills & sky. We were like two happy & rather naughty children.

"Isn't it lovely that you have come – <u>aren't we clever</u> ?"

 We lunched alone together with one dog on either side of him each in his (or her) chair, begging for his (or her) dinner. He explained how Marl Bank had been quite a vast estate in former times and showed old engravings of the huge lands and other engravings – one of Bridgnorth in Shropshire I specially liked. Most of the conversation was interspersed with dog talks, because Marco had to speak before he was given tit-bit & Mina had to conduct. There were moments when Marco would not speak in a dignified enough manner but rather too vociferously, & other times when Mina was conducting 6/8 instead of 3/4 in a bar.

So quiet & courteous & <u>un</u>fussy he was with the servants, yet he was so restless & impatient & ceaselessly active; such a gorgeous medley of Michaelangelesque grand faults & virtues. He never sat down once all the time I was there, except at the piano.

"To think we are playing together like this – isn't it a dream ?"

(It certainly seemed like one to <u>me</u> !). He had forgotten how much he liked the Sonata which henceforth he was to call My Sonata /Our Sonata.

"Isn't that a gorgeous bit – let's do it again -"

The ceiling of his drawing room was so low, the piano was so flat, but after the first few moments of embarrassment "it went." Of course he corrected various points, & speeded it up a good bit "but on the whole you understand it because you understand me and always have, before the world began." He was delirious with joy over the Romance "Oh this is such a <u>lonely</u> passage – I nearly always cry when I hear it, but I am not lonely today – we are together – I am so happy."

 Oh what a day !

After our long practice at the Sonata the rain had cleared off and there was a warm west wind with drifting grey clouds. So we took the dogs into the garden & wandered up the grassy slope to the flower garden & round into the orchard &

then down the steps on to the second lawn and into the summer house, where he worked in the warmer weather. There were old maps hanging round the walls.

We were speaking of Wagner & his orchestration & the grandeur thereof.

"But there is just one passage in the *Meistersinger* Overture – I will show you the score presently. . ." &c &c.

Here he was speaking as if I were an equal in such matters. I am afraid I pretended to be wiser than I really was when he afterwards showed me the full score. He was in such a continual state of excitement about something, hardly stopping to take breath, but always speaking in that lovely clear way with just a suspicion of the West Country in the intonation & in the sounding of "rs" which are made in our cockney English (a dismal "entertainment !")

He asked me whether I knew the Verdi *Requiem* (when I said no – "Oh I fear your ignorance is <u>abysmal</u>"). The moment we returned to the house he proceeded to put on a record of Ezio Pinza & other Italians singing *Hostias*. He marched up & down the room caged-lion fashion

"You wait a minute – it's coming."

Then when the moment came he grasped hold of my arm.

"What a voice, what divine music – oh we must have it again."

His niece Madge floated in at tea time and there was the usual routine so he told me, of tea drinking for people & cake eating for dogs. I prepared to seat myself in an armchair:

"You can't sit there, it is for Marco."

So I betook me to the couch:

"I'm afraid you can't sit there, it is for Mina."

In the end I <u>stood</u> – and fed the begging dogs with cake ! Then we adjourned to the dining room & he put on the gramophone records of his *Nursery Suite* (which I did not know then) singing and marching about so gaily while we listened & Madge smiled with tears in her eyes & said "bless him" softly under her breath.

Then we played the Sonata to her, the lovely romantic fantastic *Romance* twice over. She was delighted.

After that it was time to catch the train. They both came to the station. HE came right to the train and spoke of coming to London early next week.

Next day came this letter: –

My Dear,

Forgive this paper all I can seize as many people have rushed in. The house is still warm and alive since yesterday.

Do not forget Monday and Tuesday. I shall be as usual about 12. 15.

Ever,
E. E.

For their London meeting on Monday, 7th December, a meeting which would prove crucial to the further development of the new relationship, Elgar wanted to ensure as much quietness and privacy as possible, and Vera arranged that they would meet in her aunt's house at Carlton Hill. With its drawing-room fire glowing in the December gloom, it was the setting for their most romantic and intimate meeting so far. Elgar arrived anxious and agitated, needing the love and reassurance that only Vera, now invested with a complex of rôles, could provide. Once calm, he gave her one of the most personal gifts in his power to bestow, his mother's copy of Henry Wadsworth Longfellow's prose romance Hyperion, *whose hero's failed attempts at the realities of love are transformed into worship of an ideal Nature.*

Amid renewed talk of poetry, Elgar spoke openly and freely about his family and household and was frank about his wife's attitude to their daughter Carice, whose late marriage to an unimaginative farmer had brought her little genuine fulfilment; indeed her whole life so far had been difficult in many ways. As a child born somewhat unexpectedly perhaps to a woman in early middle age whose overwhelming preoccupation was the creative welfare of her unpredictable husband, Carice's upbringing had been very much based on the 'children should be seen and not heard' philosophy. For a good deal of the time she was not even seen, for she was sent away to board at a local school. Allowed home once a week on Sundays after Mass, she was subject even then to further instruction and correction from her mother, a major-general's daughter who expected high standards of self-discipline. Holidays were not infrequently spent with various friends and relatives while her parents were absent on musical jaunts abroad. Carice grew up a repressed, shy and dutifully obedient child, who rarely smiled or laughed, a classic victim of restrictive Victorian discipline. To make matters worse she was often unkindly teased at school over her unusual name and the dowdy clothes her mother insisted she wore. The usual childhood illnesses meant not only prolonged confinement in bed, but not even being allowed to look out of the window; and the summer months at Birchwood were, on Alice Elgar's insistence, the time for cold baths in water taken straight from the water-butt with all its creepy-crawlies. No wonder perhaps that such activities as school gymnastics paralysed Carice with fright.

But in other areas she possessed genuine abilities, although in order to preserve her father's peace and quiet, musical inclinations were not over-encouraged. Carice had been an early reader and developed a flair for languages which enabled her to work in the War Office Censorship Department during the First World War. By this time, in her mid-twenties, she had gained a suitor, a Captain Mansfield Evans. Alice Elgar, fortunately, seemed to approve, thinking him 'extremely nice,' but there was to be no happiness for Carice, for her knight in armour was killed in the last phase of the war. With the conflict over and her offical work at an end, Carice at last allowed herself a breathing space, an unprecedented period of freedom and enjoyment. At the beginning of December 1919, she went by herself on a winter sports holiday in Switzerland, and did not return until mid-March of the following year, by which time her mother was in the grip of the illness which would end her life in a matter of weeks. It was during this holiday that she met Samuel Blake, a Sussex gentleman farmer with Worcestershire antecedents who took a strong interest in her. The feeling does not seem to have been so strong on Carice's side, but various friends, fearing that she might be 'left on the shelf,' encouraged a match even though the two were perhaps not ideally suited. When Carice, now aged thirty, eventually accepted Blake's proposal, it was subject to her father's consent, and she was still so hesitant and lacking in confidence that she could not bring herself to speak to him on the matter for several days. With the consent immediately given, Carice and Sam were married quietly in London in January 1922, and went to live at his farm near Petworth. It was an ideal setting for what they had in common, a love of animals and the outdoor, countryside life.

It is a sure testament to the unthreatening warmth of Vera's personality that she and Carice were later to become lasting friends. Carice, for her part, seems to have instinctively understood and respected Vera's place in her father's world, despite her anxieties over any possible question of marriage. The two women, as good mutually supportive friends with a shared love of dogs, were remembered as sharing jokes and giggling together like schoolgirls on occasions. And there were times when it was not inconvenient for Elgar that Vera might be thought of by others as simply one of Carice's friends.

Vera's own words vividly evoke the magical sympathy which drew Elgar to her:

On Friday December 4th while he wrote me this letter I wrote him a letter of thanks for my sublime day at Worcester and for the lesson on the Sonata; also telling him that, complying with his parting request that I should try to find a quiet room where we could talk uninterruptedly in preference to the unpeaceful lounge of the Langham, I had arranged with a very sweet person – no, Person – that we might spend the afternoon in her quiet drawing room at Carlton Hill. On Saturday December 5th he wrote : –

My Dear Vera,

All thanks for your letter. All being well I shall be as usual in London at 12. 10 & shall hope to hear from you.

I am glad you have arranged for the afternoon. The dogs send love.

Your E. E.

Can you lunch at 1. 15 ?

He did arrive at mid day on Monday 7th, the first "mensiversary" of our meeting. From that day the seventh of every month was to be a festival because he knew he would not live long enough to celebrate the years.

"Of course my melodies have all 7ths – it was to be so from time immemorial," he said – regarding our meeting and his characteristic melodic leaps up or down in sevenths as mystically & prophetically interwoven.

I had given him the address & phone number at Carlton Hill. At 12. 30 precisely the telephone rang. I answered.

HE: "Oh is it really you ? Will you come & lunch with me <u>Now</u> ?"

I: "I am afraid I have promised to lunch here with my Auntie as she has to go out afterwards."

HE: "Oh dear ! Here am I going to wait until 2. 30; it is an eternity."

I: "Have patience my child the time will soon pass."

At 2. 30 He arrived rather nervous & agitated.

"I was so afraid to come in that I walked round a whole block of houses until I came back again to the same place."

He was quite perturbed. I began to comfort & reassure him just as if he were a child (" whom his mother comforteth").

"You must not feel like that when you are coming to me it is all going to be peaceful and beautiful."

It was then that he said,

"With you that most perfect threefold relationship is possible – so rare on earth. Guardian – Child – Lover."

Vera responded with the wisdom of an intelligent heart.

"And friend as well," I added.

"Yes friend too," he agreed, "and that is why I am going to give you a little book – Longfellow's *Hyperion* – which for many years belonged to my Mother. Since then for years & years it has gone with me everywhere. I want you to have it because now you are my Mother my child my lover and my friend."

By this time he had become quite calm & serene. We sat side by side on the couch in the half light gazing into the fire and sometimes into each other's eyes, and he said his happiness in that quiet room – "with you sweetness" – was so great that it must linger on there for ever.

He spoke so naturally of his "dear little wife" and of what a devoted & wonderful woman she had been but she had not understood Carice their daughter – "Carice who is so clever but alas is buried alive in a Sussex village where there is no scope for her brains and energy, but one can do nothing for her !"

So Vera was prepared in advance to understand something of Carice's life.

He spoke of his three nieces "who flit in and out of Marl Bank & who for some unknown reason are most proud of their Uncle and think that everyone who comes to see me & every letter I receive is of the utmost importance; there are no secrets from them and my secretary you understand ? "

Perhaps this is the reason that, later, Elgar and Vera would arrange to exchange letters through Carice.

Then he began to get restless again & it was rather like entertaining a volcano in a St. John's Wood drawing room.

"Let's get tea over – come on," when it was only three o'clock. I mildly suggested that it was not my house and that I thought we had better wait a little longer as the maid had her instructions.

Then he calmed down again and we spoke of poetry once more. Subsequently I must have lent him my Anthology (*Pageant of Poetry*) for he returned it to me with "7th Dec: 1931" written or bracketed against Marlowe's sonnet:

Was this the face that launched a thousand ships
And burned the topless towers of Ilium ?
<u>Oh thou art fairer than the evening air</u>
<u>Clad in the beauty of a thousand stars</u>

HE: "I have never had anyone in my life who could share everything as you can; you who know my music almost better than I do myself; who understand poetry and love nature as well, and above all who want my happiness. Others have thought it rather grand to be associated with me because of my position."

I: "I think that everything that has happened throughout my life and my love of your music has been gradual preparation for this moment, and that it was ordained we should meet in the end."

HE: "Oh my darling my sweetness." (Henceforth His name for me was sweetness; mine for him Hyperion).

We were both filled with awe-stricken wonder that it had come to pass in this strange way; that we had found one another just at sunset time – verily "an evening of extraordinary splendour."

(" . . . Thine is the tranquil hour [illegible] Eve !
But long as god like wish or hope divine informs my spirit,
Ne'er can I believe
That this magnificence is wholly thine !
From Worlds not quickened by the sun,
A portion of the gift is won.")

42

What was it about Vera that so drew Elgar to her and then held him ? She was attractive and he was susceptible. But other brief attractions did not develop into a lasting supportive friendship as this one did. The answer must lie in Vera's own strongly empathetic personality. She may have suspected that the meeting of 7th December might not be without its difficulties, but she did not avoid it. As she wrote, she recognised and understood his personality before she even met him; through his music she knew *him. Nothing showed this more clearly than the warm, motherly generosity she demonstrated that day in the protracted tête-à-tête with a nervous and intense Elgar.*

By the end of the meeting, some sort of understanding seems to have emerged about the nature of their relationship, enabling Vera to transmute what might have been a 'little flutter' into a sustaining friendship. From now on she would often be where Elgar was, not only his human spark to start a flame, but before everything, a friend.

Elgar decided to crown the day with a performance of his First Symphony at the Queen's Hall conducted by Thomas Beecham, whose reputation was as something less than a complete Elgarian. Many years before his habit of making extensive cuts in the work had become notorious. Vera – suitably dressed according to the composer's requests – was to attend with her mother.

And so the hours glided by until it was time for him to go back to the hotel to change & dine, for afterwards there was an L. S. O. concert at Queen's Hall at which Beecham was to conduct his first Symphony. "I'll just slip in at the back and hear what he makes of it." (I was going in any case.) He asked me to run upstairs and change into my black velvet frock which had made such an epoch-making impression on him at Croydon – or Corydon as he called it ("for you only have to change the order of one letter to make it <u>into such a romantic word</u>") before he left so that he might "see those arms again." It meant so much more to him than anyone I have ever known to be able to admire the exterior of someone he loved although he once said "I do not look at peoples' faces but their souls." He would gaze in a rapt manner as if he were afterwards going to take "a burning brush for Beauty's sake and limn her features whole," & then would say, "That is right I shall remember now."

Imagine those immortal hours followed by Symphony No. 1. It was a somewhat erratic performance but undoubtedly good in parts; living and fiery and unimaginably beautiful in the slow movement.

"They nearly came to grief in the last movement," said he, chuckling afterwards ! I was still sharing all his inmost intimate thoughts & dreams at Carlton Hill and here was the most wonderful dream of all ("unearthly impossible seeming"). I hardly knew whether I was there listening or still in that quiet room seated beside him in the firelight

"As a spirit who has dwelt within his heart of hearts . . .

and known

The inmost converse of his Soul
I have unlocked the golden melodies
Of his deep soul and bathed myself therein –
Even as an eagle in a thunder mist
Clothing his wings with lightning."

It was discovered that He was in the hall and there was a great commotion until he appeared, when the whole audience rose as one man and uproariously acclaimed him.

When he was bowing to the public, he suddenly caught sight of me near the front of the stalls & such a wonderful look of recognition came into his eyes and he beckoned & pointed with his right hand to the Artists' room, indicating that I was to take Mother to be introduced to him.

Gradually Elgar and Vera introduced each other to more and more friends and relatives. Next day, Tuesday 8th December, he took her to see the elderly Adela Schuster, the sister of one of his earliest and most influential friends and supporters outside Worcestershire circles, Frank Schuster. The Schusters had been able to introduce Elgar to a wider literary, artistic and social world. Adela herself had been an intimate friend and supporter of Oscar Wilde, offering him any help within her power on his arrest. She subsequently sent him a cheque for a thousand pounds with the assurance that it was a wholly inadequate recognition of the pleasure his conversation had given her. Wilde wrote of her as 'the lady of Wimbledon,' and thought her 'one of the most beautiful personalities I have ever known.' Vera's pen portrait of her is a memorable vignette. Then at Elgar's request they went to Shirley Park so Vera could show him the hotel where she was temporarily living, set in a beautiful expanse of woodland and open country that was once a royal hunting-ground. Shirley House, as it once was, dated from the 1720s and had associations with Carlyle, Ruskin, and Thackeray. Elgar would have been intrigued to know that in the late eighteenth century it had witnessed a pitched battle between a party of smugglers and dragoons, who captured five horses laden with contraband destined for Croydon. During the visit, Vera introduced him to her eleven year-old daughter Dulcie; John was away at school in Berkshire, from where he would gain a scholarship to read History at Jesus College, Cambridge. Although it was said of Elgar that he was not the kind of man who was naturally fond of children, there was an immediate rapport with Dulcie and the composer would write her many affectionate letters, punningly if rather pointedly signing himself 'Dead-wood' Elgar. The following year she would be the subject of a classic Elgarian jape, agreeing to sign a contract for the supply of the requisite amount of notes, dots and rests for the Third Symphony.

On the drive to Shirley the composer revealed how flattered he was by Shaw's admiration, and gave one of the most succinct summings-up that we have on documentary record of his views not only on the light music versus serious music debate – 'I prefer good Delibes to bad Brahms' – but over the Royal College of Music as well.

Next day it was arranged that I should go to the Langham & together we were to drive to Wimbledon to see a wonderful old lady, Miss Schuster, sister of his great friend, (deceased.)

"I have told her I am bringing the sweetest person in the world to see her."

She was reclining on a couch, very tall & gaunt & silver-haired & frail & ancient looking – with only her dark eyes youthful & ablaze with passionate intelligence – in an old world faded-chintz drawing-room, the walls lined with book cases all filled with book treasures, with large French windows opening on to a huge garden.

It struck me so strange that my wondrous Being (glorious Hyperion) should be a contemporary of this aged lady and that they should be sharing reminiscences of a certain remote evening spent in company of "Matt Arnold" and R.L.S. – yet it was ever so charming to see their genuine love for each other – "Do you remember that day on the river, Edward," etc. He seemed to put fresh life into her and she was just as deeply learned as he, they seemed to know all that there is to be known about English Literature. They both had prodigious memories for everything that had ever interested them. She was undoubtedly the champion when it came to quotations. I sat very mouse-like, putting in an occasional word when some poem was discussed that I happened to know. But I did not feel strange for one moment because his love for me had transformed me into the someone I had always longed to be; small and insignificant but with the power of bringing divine happiness into the life of a giant !

We took leave of the wonderful Lady and drove from Wimbledon to Shirley Park Hotel in order that he might see where I lived. I remember en route He spoke of G.B.S.

"Fancy that wonderman thinks I am a greater man than he !" (As if there were any doubt !) We sang together endless subjects of favourite Symphonies, &c & it was then that he invented "Vera's scrap heap" upon which to throw all works which were "manufactured" and not truly inspired:

"I must have the best of everything: I prefer good Delibes to bad Brahms, but of course you have a Royal College mind and think all light music is bad music."

I am sorry to say Brahms's D Major and C Minor Symphonies were thrown on the heap there & then, together with the *Requiem* [and] the Bach B Minor Mass. He <u>groaned</u> at my abysmal ignorance each time I was unfamiliar with Meyerbeer, Donnizetti & Delibes tunes !

"Oh what a lovely park," he exclaimed, looking at that great expanse of velvety greenness, with the bare woods of Shirley beyond, fading away into the sunset sky.

He was introduced to Dulcie & soon they were sitting with their heads together, talking of schooldays & schoolmistresses & of course lovely tales of Marco & Mina. She heard about his young days when he was expected to go round in a top hat & frock coat, teaching at a young ladies' Seminary. One day he arrived in shooting breeches equivalent to our plus fours.

"Rather athletic, Mr. Elgar?" came the acid voice of the headmistress from behind a rose bush.

"<u>Very</u>," he agreed.

He teased her; she reciprocated. She could not be shy. It seemed the most natural thing in the world to have the Master of the King's Musick in our bed-sitting room – the room with a view – talking nonsense.

"What a sweet child; I never remember seeing a sweeter; she is a radiant part of you."

And it was said of Dulcie in later life that she had the same gift her mother had, of making whoever she was speaking to feel a special centre of attention and sympathy. Elgar returned to Marl Bank and wrote to Vera next day.

10th December.

Sweetest and Dearest,

I got back safely & wish I had not left. It was a restful and a happy time all the time. Please write and tell me all.

I fear the little book Hyperion is not worth your notice but it is or was, a piece of me and now we share.

Love ever,

E.

And the next day, he wrote again, with another intimate gift. Once more, the message was self-deprecating in a way that takes us to the heart of the composer's nature. The last sentence especially, with its unique Elgarian cadences, marks a most touching tribute of his love for Vera.

Then on December 11th accompanying the MS of the Violin & Piano Sonata (& against his signature at the end he put "<u>who only now knows why this was written</u>.")

For the New Year I wanted to send something; of course nothing of the slightest value. In the packet are all the existing sketches of your Sonata. I would not wait till the last day of this dying wonderful year so here is the waste paper now.

Ever,

E. E.

And there, just over a month after their first meeting, Vera's account comes to an end. Just one further fragment of documentary evidence from this period survives, a page from the Shirley Park Hotel's message pad with a telegram for 'Mrs Hockman' from 'Hyperion.' It is dated 12th December, 1931, the day after the gift of the Violin Sonata sketches, and in it Elgar announced his intention to come to Vera again the following Tuesday, 15th December. The pattern of their meetings would continue, albeit in a less documented way, for Elgar did not cease to cherish his new muse, whose inspiration would bring him so tantalisingly close to the achievement of the three planned major works of his old age.

Elgar, Billy Reed and Alan Kirby at Croydon, 7th November 1931

Alan Kirby

Croydon Baths Hall

THE HIGH STREET, CROYDON.

C.A.P. Co. 494A.

Croydon High Street, with Grants on the right

The Shirley Park Hotel, formerly Shirley House

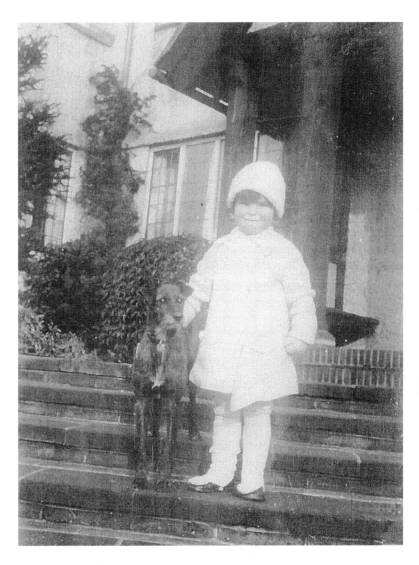

Dulcie and her Song

21. THE WORLD'S A BUBBLE

The World's a bubble, and the Life of Man
Less than a span;
In his conception wretched, from the womb
So to the tomb;
Curst from his cradle, and brought up to years
With cares and fears.
Who then to frail mortality shall trust,
But limns on water, or but writes in dust.

FRANCIS BACON, LORD VERULAM.

22. LUCIFER'S SONG

Thou hast more music in thy voice
Than to the spheres is given,
And more temptations on thy lips
Than lost the angels Heaven.
Thou hast more brightness in thine eyes
Than all the stars which burn,
More dazzling art thou than the throne
We fallen dared to spurn.

Go, search through Heaven—the sweetest smile
That lightens there is thine;
And through hell's burning darkness breaks
No frown so fell as mine.
One smile—'twill light, one tear—'twill cool;
These will be more to me
Than all the wealth of all the worlds,
Or boundless power could be.

P. J. BAILEY (*Festus*).

23. WE LIVE IN DEEDS

We live in deeds, not years; in thoughts, not breaths;
In feelings, not in figures on a dial.
We should count time by heart-throbs. He most lives
Who thinks most, feels the noblest, acts the best.
Where imperfection ceaseth, heaven begins.

P. J. BAILEY (*Festus*).

24. FISHERMAN'S SONG

No fish stir in our heaving net,
And the sky is dark and the night is wet;
And we must ply the lusty oar,
For the tide is ebbing from the shore;
And sad are they whose faggots burn,
So kindly stored for our return.

Our boat is small, and the tempest raves,
And nought is heard but the lashing waves
And the sullen roar of the angry sea,
And the wild winds piping drearily;
Yet sea and tempest rise in vain,
We'll bless our blazing hearths again.

Push bravely, mates! Our guiding star
Now from its towered streameth far,
And now along the nearing strand,
See, swiftly moves yon flaming brand.
Before the midnight watch be past
We'll quaff our bowl and mock the blast.

JOANNA BAILLIE.

25. LIFE! I KNOW NOT WHAT THOU ART

Life! I know not what thou art,
But know that thou and I must part;
And when, or how, or where we met
I own to me's a secret yet.

Life! we've been long together
Through pleasant and through cloudy weather;
'Tis hard to part when friends are dear—
Perhaps 'twill cost a sigh, a tear;
—Then steal away, give little warning,
Choose thine own time;
Say not Good Night,—but in some brighter clime
Bid me Good Morning.

A. L. BARBAULD.

26. SPRING

Sweet daughter of a rough and stormy sire,
Hoar Winter's blooming child, delightful Spring!
Whose unshorn locks with leaves
And swelling buds are crowned;

From the green islands of eternal youth
(Crowned with fresh blooms, and ever-springing shade),
Turn, hither turn thy step,
O thou, whose powerful voice,
More sweet than softest touch of Doric reed,
Or Lydian flute, can soothe the madding winds,
And through the stormy deep
Breathe thy own tender calm.

Sweet is thy reign, but short: the red dogstar
Shall scorch thy tresses; and the mower's scythe
Thy greens, thy flowerets all,
Remorseless shall destroy.

Reluctant shall I bid thee then farewell;
For O! not all that Autumn's lap contains,
Nor Summer's ruddiest fruits,
Can aught for thee atone,

Fair Spring! whose simplest promise more delights,
Than all their largest wealth, and through the heart
Each joy and new-born hope
With softest influence breathes.

A. L. BARBAULD (*Ode to Spring*).

That Faustus may repent and save his soul!
O lente, lente currite, noctis equi!
The stars move still, time runs, the clock will strike,
The devil will come, and Faustus must be damned.
O, I'll leap up to my God!—Who pulls me down?—
See, see, where Christ's blood streams in the firmament!—
One drop would save my soul, half a drop: ah, my Christ!—
Ah, rend not my heart for naming of my Christ!—
Yet will I call on Him: O, spare me, Lucifer!—
Where is it now? 'tis gone: and see, where God
Stretcheth out His arm, and bends His ireful brows!
Mountains and hills, come, come, and fall on me,
And hide me from the heavy wrath of God!
No, no!
Then will I headlong run into the earth:
Earth, gape! O, no, it will not harbour me
You stars that reigned at my nativity,
Whose influence hath allotted death and hell,
Now draw up Faustus, like a foggy mist,
Into the entrails of yon labouring clouds,
That, when you vomit forth into the air,
My limbs may issue from your smoky mouths,
So that my soul may but ascend to heaven!
           C. MARLOWE (*Faustus*).

638. THE PASSIONATE SHEPHERD TO HIS LOVE

Come live with me and be my love,
And we will all the pleasures prove
That hills and valleys, dale and field,
And all the craggy mountains yield.

There will we sit upon the rocks
And see the shepherds feed their flocks,
By shallow rivers, to whose falls
Melodious birds sing madrigals.

And I will make thee beds of roses
And a thousand fragrant posies,
A cap of flowers, and a kirtle
Embroidered all with leaves of myrtle.

A gown made of the finest wool,
Which from our pretty lambs we pull,
Fair linèd slippers for the cold,
With buckles of the purest gold.

A belt of straw and ivy buds
With coral clasps and amber studs:
And if these pleasures may thee move,
Come live with me and be my love.

The shepherd swains shall dance and sing
For thy delight each May-morning:
If these delights thy mind may move,
Then live with me and be my love.
           C. MARLOWE.[1]

639. WHO EVER LOVED, THAT LOVED NOT AT FIRST SIGHT?

It lies not in our power to love or hate,
For will in us is overruled by fate.
When two are stripped, long ere the course begin,
We wish that one should lose, the other win;
And one especially do we affect
Of two gold ingots, like in each respect:
The reason no man knows; let it suffice
Where we behold is censured by our eyes.
Where both deliberate, the love is slight:
Who ever loved, that loved not at first sight?
           C. MARLOWE (*Hero and Leander*).

640. HELEN

Was this the face that launched a thousand ships,
And burned the topless towers of Ilium?—
Sweet Helen, make me immortal with a kiss!—
Her lips suck forth my soul: see where it flees!—
Come, Helen, come, give me my soul again.
Here will I dwell, for heaven is in these lips,
And all is dross that is not Helena.
I will be Paris, and for love of thee,
Instead of Troy, shall Wittenberg be sacked,
And I will combat with weak Menelaus,
And wear thy colours on my plumèd crest;
Yes, I will wound Achilles in the heel,
And then return to Helen for a kiss.
Oh, thou art fairer than the evening air
Clad in the beauty of a thousand stars;—
Brighter art thou than flaming Jupiter
When he appeared to hapless Semele;
More lovely than the monarch of the sky
In wanton Arethusa's azured arms;
And none but thou shalt be my paramour!
           C. MARLOWE (*Faustus*).

[1] See Ralegh's reply, No. 771.

Two pages from Vera's *Pageant of English Poetry*, with Elgar's markings

'In remembrance Croydon Festival 1931'

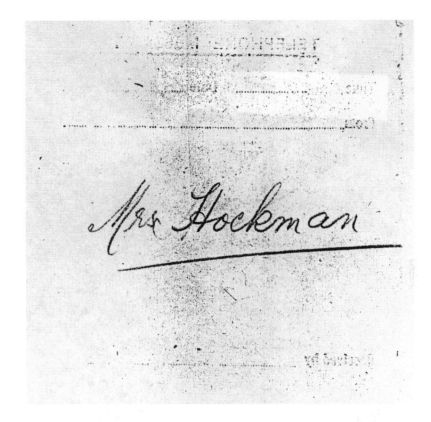

Mrs Hockman

TELEPHONE·MESSAGE.

Time _12·5 PM_ Date _12/12/31_
From _Worcester_ _11·16 am_

Many thanks.
Tuesday morning.
Am writing.

Hyperion

Received by _Hall Porter_

A message from Hyperion

Vera's house, Robin Hill

Vera with her children, mother and grandparents

Portrait study of Carice

Portrait study of Carice

Elgar arriving with Carice for her wedding at St. James's Church, Spanish
Place, London on 16th January, 1922

Carice and Sam Blake on their honeymoon. 'My daughter has no dress sense,'
Elgar is said to have remarked on one occasion

Chapter 2   V. H.'s Own Theme

Do not go gentle into that good night,
Old age should burn and rave at close of day;
Rage, rage against the dying of the light.

Dylan Thomas

Elgar passed Christmas quietly at Marl Bank with Arthur Troyte Griffith and his daughter Carice, who noted in her diary that the composer listened to records of three of the Schumann symphonies – music full of exhilarating romantic verve – on Boxing Day afternoon. But on 29th December he wrote to Ernest Newman in a way which seemed to draw a deliberate mask over his new-found relationship: '...naturally, you are in my thoughts more than anyone connected with music... You will easily understand that my interest in our art is now very slight or, perhaps, I shd. say, dead...I am clearing things up for an early 'demise'...I live here alone with my dogs & rarely go to London & my visits to town are for necy. busines...'

In the new year he received a letter from Bernard Shaw, en route for South Africa aboard the steamer *Carnarvon Castle*. The friendship of composer and playwright had progressed to frankness over financial matters and sometime during the previous year Shaw had lent Elgar the sum of £1,000 – well over £30,000 at today's values – to alleviate his anxieties over money, anxieties which had been a lifelong characteristic although not always strictly borne out by the style in which he lived. Certainly Elgar had seen his income diminish in the harsh economic climate of the twenties. But in a characteristically impulsive gesture he had bought outright, not rented, his atmospheric old three-storey, nine-bedroomed Worcester house, Marl Bank, a house he had known from childhood, with almost two acres of gardens and grounds and views of Worcester Cathedral and the Malvern Hills. Its upkeep proved a burden at times, particularly when gales blew down a substantial section of garden wall. Shaw concluded his letter with a hint that renewed large-scale composition – a symphony – might offer a financial way forward: 'You know, times are not really bad. It is this silly pauperizing plundering of Germany to send money to France and America without any return trade, and paying it all in gold which has enabled those two highly undeserving countries to corner all the gold, which America hoards, that has deadlocked the commercial machine. Meanwhile, however, they keep playing Land of Hope and Glory, Salut d'Amour, and the Wand of Youth. Why dont you make the B.B.C. order a new symphony? It can afford it.' So the hint was well and truly given, although Elgar himself might seem the last person to want to 'make' such arrangements. Shaw's own experience as a practical man-of-the-world would be vital in creating the BBC commission. But any more intimate creative rôle in the music on his part has surely been exaggerated. That belonged to Vera.

For there can be little doubt that in the wake of his new-found love Elgar was coming alive again, and showing every interest in the continued resumption of creative work, especially on the symphony. Ernest Newman visited Marl Bank for a few days in the middle of January and wrote that he found the composer 'very fit.' He treasured, too, some manuscript sketches of the symphony that Elgar gave him, even at that early stage. Wulstan Atkins, who saw the composer regularly at weekends for most of the next two years, was vividly aware of the new energy emanating from him. Elgar seemed to live less in the past and Atkins wrote that his 'country gentleman' attitude 'seemed to be changing to something more vital and positive.' As if to keep his hand in, the composer spent the first part of 1932 making an orchestral version of the *Severn Suite,* but it was evident to Atkins that work was under way on a variety of projects – an opera, *The Spanish Lady,* a piano concerto, and the third part of *The Apostles* – as well as the symphony. Gradually the study at Marl Bank filled with manuscript sketches, kept in piles on the piano, or sometimes pinned to bookcases or curtains for Billy Reed to play from, as he had for work on the Violin Concerto of over twenty years before. The symphony seemed to be taking over, although Atkins found it difficult to make sense of the sketches because of their apparently unconnected nature. 'The only thing that was clear,' he wrote, ' was that Elgar's creative genius was again taking control and driving him on.'

Vera's continuing presence would have sustained such a mood, although there is little enough documentary evidence of further meetings at this point. Some time in February she was presented with a signed miniature score of the Second Symphony, and at the end of March she was present at a Worcester dinner where Elgar made a speech. The occasion was recorded in Carice's diary, which now becomes not only the major source of information about Elgar and Vera, but reveals a great deal about her own little-known, devoted efforts on her father's behalf amidst her responsibilities as the wife of a busy and increasingly unwell Sussex farmer. If Elgar told Vera that he thought there was no scope for Carice's brains and energy in her village, she certainly found an outlet in the frequent long drives she undertook to assist in her father's activities, to say nothing of the letters she wrote in answer to his frequent complaints over day-to-day problems of health and domestic matters:

Thursday 31 March 1932. Left home about 10. Did shopping in Petworth & on to Guildford. Left about 1.30 & got to Worcester about 3. 30. Went off to dinner at 7 – Vera, Billie, Mr Norman Forbes Sir Hugh Allen & many known from Worcester. Father made good speeches – amusing evening.

That spring a typically Elgarian 'jape' was hatched for Dulcie, away at boarding school in Sussex, to be pressed into service in aid of the symphony. She would have to sign a contract for the supply of all the required notes and rests in time for the composer's seventy-fifth birthday in June. Elgar told her:

> I shall require strings and strings of semiquavers, demisemiquavers and of course all the other kinds of notes, also rests, dots, etc. You go out and catch them in a butterfly net and then hang them out to dry for a considerable time – and don't forget to include a pair of scissors and a paste pot because I usually compose by cutting out other people's music and pasting it on to my own.

And the contract was duly drawn up and agreed:

> I, Dulcie, agree to supply the required quantity of notes, rests, dots, etc. Also scissors and a paste pot to be despatched to Edward Elgar by June 2nd, 1932.

That was his seventy-fifth birthday; it was a busy, happy day, no doubt with Vera's participation in one form or another:

> Thursday 2 June 1932. Father's 75th birthday. Lovely day. Hectic morning – telephone, telegrams etc. etc. To see Father off by 12 train & round town. Very good spirits.

In accordance with her contract, Dulcie carefully cut out many notes and rests from some of her oldest pieces of music and sent them off in batches. The result was a page of score despatched to Dulcie on Midsummer Day containing a self-portrait of the distracted composer surrounded by a nightmare collection of misbehaving music. The number of beats in a bar varied from 15 to 42; there were long sustained bass notes for the flutes and double-bass patterns high in the treble stave; clarinets were pitched 'in trouble' and horns 'in strawhats'; the side-drum played *Salut d'Amour* pianissimo while a cat chased some mice along the double-bassoon stave and a jug poured water into some glasses where the second clarinet part should have been. Two blots were converted into insects by the addition of legs – the smaller one being presumably the lesser of two weevils. In the bottom right-hand corner there was a note for Dulcie:

> I am sorry to say that the materials you sent <u>& charged for</u> are intractable & I have found it necessary to scrap the entire consignment & retire to a nursing home to recover. Yours Affectionately, Edward Elgar.

Vera added a note of explanation when the page of score was displayed at a School exhibition.

On the appointed day Dulcie sent off strings and strings of notes, dots, rests as ordered, nor did she forget to include the account, together with a few words of advice as to how a beginner should set about composing a Symphony and what pitfalls to avoid. But alas! the consignment failed to meet with Edward Elgar's approval. They were old stock ("possibly suitable to the second-rate stuff I turn out nowadays") and quite intractable, all the wrong notes for the wrong instruments. But the contract had been signed so the only thing to do was to grin and bear it and despatch a cheque signed by Marco, Mina and Mobey, Edward Elgar's three dogs.

For Elgar, as he said, Dulcie was part of Vera and they enjoyed a warmly affectionate 'Wand of Youth' relationship across the generations. He wrote her many letters which, according to family legend, subsequently disappeared without trace after having been sent to a researcher who asked to see them.

But despite the whimsicality, Elgar evidently felt serious enough about a new symphony to broach the matter to his publishers, Keith Prowse, during a visit to London that month. When the critic Ferrucio Bonavia suggested that Elgar score the Chopin Bb minor sonata in order to make a symphony, the composer responded that he would rather write one of his own. At the end of June, Shaw again wrote to encourage the symphony, emphasizing anew the financial aspect. Now that Elgar was Shaw's debtor, the playwright had some legitimate cause for feeling that Elgar's financial interest was his own, and one may perhaps be forgiven for wondering whether a knife was very gently being twisted. 'Why not a Financial Symphony?' he wrote. 'Allegro: Impending Disaster. Lento mesto: Stony Broke. Scherzo: Light Heart and Empty Pocket. Allo. con brio: Clouds Clearing.' And as the summer wore on, talk of the new symphony began to filter through the musical world, although Elgar was deliberately and characteristically discouraging in reply to a direct question from Walter Legge, editor of *The Voice* magazine: ' . . . there is nothing to say about the mythical Symphony for some time, – probably a long time, – possibly no time, – never.' But Wulstan Atkins remembered that it was on his visit to Marl Bank on 14th August that year, that he heard Elgar for the first time playing sketches specifically referred to as being for the Third Symphony.

With the London rehearsals for that year's Three Choirs Festival at Worcester, Elgar's relationship with Vera comes somewhat more fully into documentary view once more. Carice, who had recently taken proud possession of a new Hillman Minx, drove up from Petworth to take Vera to meet Elgar at the Royal College of Music for a rehearsal of *The Music Makers,* one of the six Elgar works on the programme:

Tuesday, 30 August. Left early – & went to Vera's at Croydon – car did its 500 en route. Lunch with her – & took her up to RCM in car – great thrill – heard rehearsal & saw Father . . . Back to Robin Hill about 7.

Carice stayed with Vera for two nights altogether. Next day there was another venture up to town including, in a further extension of the family friendship, lunch with Vera's mother:

Wednesday, 31 August. Up to RCM again in car – & took Vera & Mrs. Brown – Nice time – Lunch with Mrs. Marks (Vera's mother) & to tea with Mrs. Johnasson – Miss Tweed there. Hair washed etc at Harrod's – back to Vera about 7. 30.

It was a hectic period for Carice. She returned home for one day and then drove to Worcester for the Festival week, collecting Vera, who was to join Elgar's house-party at Marl Bank. They arrived to find the Shaws and their friend the former Lawrence of Arabia – a sincere admirer of Elgar's music – assembled ready to listen to the test pressings of the Violin Concerto, which he had recorded in July with Yehudi Menuhin:

Friday, 2nd September. Got off about 9. 30 – eventually left Petworth at 10. Got to Reading at 11. 25, met Vera – picnic lunch near Woodstock – got to Worcester at 4 – large party – Mr. & Mrs. G. B. S. & Col. Lawrence now known as Shaw – Dr. Palmer's brother brought him over – '

At this Worcester Festival, his last, Elgar did not find it necessary to propose to set impossible words or launch into public argument with local worthies of the church. His new-found zest for life was reflected in his 'open house' at Marl Bank and in his enthusiastic, cheerful presence at a variety of events, musical and social. According to Wulstan Atkins, he was 'in wonderful form.' Next day Vera would have shared in the enjoyment of a wonderful surprise planned by Ivor Atkins and Billy Reed:

Saturday 3 September 1932. In town in am. Rehearsal in pm saw many people. Sir Ivor gave an organ recital in pm. Billy played slow movement of Violin Concerto with organ accpt. Whole thing beautifully done. Just a few people invited. Cathedral dark except for floodlighting.

It was a memorable introduction to an historic Festival week. Elgar conducted *The Dream of Gerontius* on the Tuesday, the First Symphony – Vera was presented with an autographed score – and the eagerly awaited première of the orchestral version of the *Severn Suite* (which the *Sunday Pictorial* referred to as 'The Severn Sweet,' no doubt much to its composer's delight) on the Wednesday. *The Music Makers* and *For The Fallen* followed on the Thursday. That day Carice went to the Lord Mayor's lunch with her Aunt Pollie and Vera and on the following day, Friday, she noted that Harold Brooke of Novello's 'came up & took more films.' Elgar had attended the then customary Friday morning performance of *Messiah*, but he evidently decided to miss the afternoon performance of his Piano Quintet with Myra Hess and the Griller Quartet. Instead he spent time that sunny afternoon with Vera and other members of the house party at Marl Bank. The images that Harold Brooke captured of them that day remain, together with *The Story of November 7th, 1931*, among the most revealing and touching documents of Vera and her relationship with the composer. The film captures perfectly the interaction between them as she emerges from the house together with Carice and the secretary Mary Clifford, gracefully moving towards him with a characteristic, very feminine little run, talking to him and gazing into his face.

Elgar was evidently in no hurry to let Vera depart after the Festival week and she stayed on for several days before leaving with Carice. There were opportunities for her to be shown round the composer's own landscape with Billy Reed and to meet Arthur Troyte Griffith. And Elgar very much wanted Vera to see the place that was most important to him of all the houses where he had lived, the tiny cottage at Broadheath where he had been born, the beginning of his creative life. Vera would return there several times in later years.

Saturday 10 September 1932. Fine am. Billy took us in the town in am. & we went on to Broadheath for dogs' run & saw over Father's birthplace – labourer's cottage now – very sweet. They said they had had lots of people looking over during the last week. Wonderful drive in pm. Billy's car & mine – & we changed passengers. Stonehall Common, Castlemorton & tea in a cottage at Castlemorton – Tewkesbury, Pershore, Evesham. Home just after 8 – had my lights on for first time.

Sundays often saw Carice going to church – she remained a practising Catholic – while her father went to work on the *Observer* crossword puzzle. It was another sign of a continuing active mind:

Sunday 11 September 1932. Wet early but nice later. May & I to Church at 8. Puzzle difficult. Drive in am to common & call on Troyte. Promised to fetch him after lunch. May Vera & I went – he stayed to tea and dinner. Billy took him back after. Vera Father & I went – lovely moon.

Monday 12 September 1932. All in town in am. Billy left after lunch. Took car down to have greasing etc. that was necessary after 1500 miles. Vera Father & I drive after tea to Hanbury Common – lovely there. Records after dinner.

Tuesday 13 September 1932. Wet early but fine later. All went to Mr Willis Bund's sale & stayed till 12. Gloomy house. Father bought some glass.

Went to Bank & Vera & I left about 12. 45. Picnic lunch & got to Robin Hill about 6. 45, via Henley, Wargrave, Virginia Water. Got rather lost by Esher but found way all right.

Wednesday 14 September 1932. Lovely day, sitting out. Walk in woods with Vera. Left after lunch – got in about 4.30. Busy unpacking etc. Sam to Findon Fair – home about 6. Dogs very pleased to be home.

It must have been a memorable period for Vera, and some eight years later, looking back from the strange vantage-point of the Christmas of 1940, she wrote another memoir of Elgar, with the RCM rehearsal as its starting-point and her departure from Marl Bank after the Festival as its conclusion. There was a certain amount of anecdotal material, some familiar, some new, but essentially the document was a record of the conversations Vera and Elgar had shared about his music and the poetry which might relate closely to it, with various examples. She called it *Elgar & Poetry* and headed it with a quotation from *The Music Makers*.

> We are the Music Makers
> And we are the dreamers of dreams
> Wandering by lone sea-breakers
> And sitting by desolate streams.
>
> ....
>
> A breath of our inspiration
> Is the life of each generation,
> A wondrous thing of our dreaming,
> Unearthly, impossible seeming . . .

"Do you think it was very vainglorious of me to quote my own dreams in *The Music Makers*?" asked E. E.

"I think it glorious in you, not vainglorious, to have the vision that penetrates the thin veil of the present, so that you can see your own immortality revealed," I said.

We were dining at the Langham Hotel after a long day of rehearsals for the Three Choirs Festival (held at the Royal College of Music) at which Muriel Brunskill had given a memorable performance of the contralto solo part in the *Music Makers*. It had been my first experience of this work and I had been deeply moved, but not surprised, as E. E.'s own dreams came floating past whenever the dreamers of dreams are mentioned throughout the work. Arthur O'Shaughnessy's poem had a particularly intimate significance for Elgar, for his own soul was so steeped in poetry that he could not help identifying himself with the "one man on whose soul it hath broken, a light that doth not depart . . ."

Was it not prophetic that Elgar quoted the *Nimrod* Variation in this context, seeing that nowadays it has become an almost established convention, at solemn moments in our national life, or when announcing the passing of a great soul, to play *Nimrod*?

The Music Makers is not great poetry perhaps – E. E. used to say that it is better to set the best second rate poetry to music for the most immortal verse <u>is</u> Music already – but it expresses the grand theme that the poets and dreamers are the real movers and shakers of the world, and ultimately the shapers of its destiny.

And Shelley himself had written, 'Poets are the unacknowledged legislators of the world.' Vera continued with some of Elgar's reminiscences of the first stirrings of his need for expression, a need that was perceived before the right vehicle for it was apparent. Literature had been as important as music to him, and the two remained closely linked. Eventually he could not help but choose music, although he 'never really wanted to be a musician' and once told Sir Hubert Parry that the only honour he really wanted was that of D. Litt. Elgar described his feelings about his creative process from beginning to end, and Vera added his by now predictable reaction to any suggestion of 'Enigmatising.'

To his own intimate circle of friends and relations Elgar was quite frank about his greatness:

"From the time I was a boy, rummaging about among the books in my father's loft, I knew I was going to create something lasting; whether it was to be in the realm of literature or music I did not know, but I felt the creative force stirring within me . . . I never really wanted to be a musician, for nobody wanted music at that time, but I couldn't help it . . . You have to give birth to musical ideas; a slow process of gestation, then come the birth pangs, but once the composition has been brought into the world it is no longer a part of you. You look on it quite objectively as a mother looks upon the off-spring as a new being she has somehow miraculously produced."

Poetry was always in the background of his mind; poetry of all ages, with the exception of the very modern; and perhaps it is for this reason that while listening to his work I have often found that a poem I have known and loved detaches itself from some almost forgotten haunt in the memory and seems to keep pace with the music just as the shadow melody is alleged to "go with the theme" in the Enigma Variations.

If this subject of the Enigma were mentioned, E. E. would purse up his lips and look sphinx-like, with eyes twinkling all the time, but never a word would he say!

Vera, whose responses to music and literature were as intense and as intuitive as Elgar's, went on to suggest extracts from various poems that she felt to be related to particular passages in his music.

Sometimes, while quietly talking over the music, as on the occasion mentioned above, I have suggested to E. E. the poem which seemed to me to be the counterpart of a particular movement, variation, or interlude. Take for instance the Finale of the Second Symphony, sweeping along with bold, majestic rhythm. These are the words that came: –

So we must laugh and drink from the deep blue cup of the sky,
Join the jubilant song of the great stars sweeping by,
Laugh and battle and work, and drink of the wine outpoured
In the dear green earth the sign of the joy of the Lord.

Laugh and be merry together like brothers akin
Guesting awhile in the rooms of a beautiful inn . . .

There is Orion striding across the sky, the red gem Betelgeuse on his shoulder, bright jewels shining in his belt; Sirius, the dog star, follows behind glitteringly dazzlingly silver and blue and white. The Hyades and the Plyades too – the jubilant song of the stars!   Then after the triumphant procession of the constellations the movement slows down to that soft, wistful close.

  Glad till the dancing stops, the lilt of the music ends.

"Yes, that will do," he said, (with E. E. it was always " it will do" or " it won't do – I don't want it," and that was final.) "And I like to hear the name Betelgeuse – say it again!"

Betelgeuse is a star thought to be three times hotter than the Sun. Astronomy was another close interest of Vera's.

The *Nimrod* Variation.

E. E. often told one proudly that Richard Strauss had said to him,
"This is the longest sustained climax in music, Edward; how do you do it? I can't."
What verse spiritual enough to go side by side with it? This is the vision that came to me: -
The poet stands motionless upon that silent hill in the profound stillness, staring up into the sky ("the sky was lit, the sky was stars all over it"). Suddenly

the sound of distant music; it comes nearer and nearer, flooding his soul, the Song of Honour, welling up from every living creature and ascending to the throne of God. The still, small, soft, sustained opening of *Nimrod*, then the gradual, mighty crescendo: –

I heard the Universal choir
The Sons of Light exalt their Sire,
Earth's lowliest and loudest notes,
Her million times ten million throats
Exalt him loud and long . . .

I heard it all, I heard the whole
Harmonious hymn of being roll
Up through the chapel of my soul,
And in the awful quiet then
Myself I heard, Amen, Amen . . .

The wonder of beautiful verses or of human or animal form, or of lovely landscape (the Malvern Hills, outlined hyacinthine-blue against the evening sky, the noble cathedral tower in the mid-distance) never ceased to move him to ecstasy, as if experienced for the first time, – Eden new, we used to say, quoting Alfred Noyes. Certain lines would reduce him to tears again and again:

As you came from the Holy land of Walsingham
Met you not with my true love
By the way as you came?

"It's no use, I can't say it without crying. 'As you came from the Holy land of Walsingham met you not with my true love . . .' "

The tears would invariably come.

The poem, thought to be by Sir Walter Ralegh, referred to a pilgrimage to Mary the Egyptian, the medieval patron saint of lovers, at Walsingham. Significantly, the lines affirm an old man's belief that 'true love is a durable fire' despite the indifference of his former, younger mistress.

Other lines he would repeat to himself softly, chuckling with the joy of them. Of these, 'Thoughts in a Garden' by Andrew Marvell were a supreme example, and I often wonder whether they were in his subconscious mind when he composed those two exquisite, gossamer-woven interludes from Falstaff:

Meanwhile the mind from pleasure less
Withdraws into its happiness.
The mind, that ocean where each kind
Does straight its own resemblance find;
Yet it creates, transcending these
Far other worlds and other seas,
Annihilating all that's made
To a green thought in a green shade.

"A green thought in a green shade" – Shallow's orchard!

The *Introduction and Allegro.*

The Introduction and Allegro suggests the sea dashing against a rugged and rocky coast, the sea gulls swirling and poising and crying.

The accumulated murmur of soft plashing
Of waves on rocks dashing and searching the sands
Takes my ear in the veering
Baffled winds, as rearing
Upright at the cliff, to the gullies and rifts he stands
And his conquering surges scour out over the lands
While again at the foot of the Downs
He masses his strength, to recover the topmost crowns.

Then there is the more strident and flamboyant mood of the Pomp and Circumstance Marches.

The Princes applaud with a furious joy
The Many rend the skies with loud appplause.

He loved to declaim those strong triumphant lines from Dryden's "Alexander's Feast," throwing back his head and smiling his conquering smile. I feel they rather correspond with Elgar's characteristic use of the brass!

When considering the Violin Concerto, that most passionate and intimate work and one with a private relationship at its heart, Vera felt some lines from Shelley to be appropriate. But first she went back to the day of her arrival at Marl Bank, Friday 2nd September, to paint a memorable picture of the scene as the company listened for the first time to the young Menuhin's wonderful recording. Vera also quoted from a letter Elgar had written to her which might show that he was warming again to the experiences behind the music. She revealed that he was inclined to think the concerto his most inspired work, and that the doubts about Menuhin's suitability which he had previously shared with her had been triumphantly erased.

I shall never hear the Slow Movement of the Violin Concerto without recalling a scene at Marl Bank in September, 1932 in the dining room where the gramophone and records were kept. There was gathered together a small circle of intimate friends, among them Mr. & Mrs. G. B. Shaw, Aircraftman Shaw, alias Lawrence of Arabia, his daughter, Mrs. Elgar Blake, and of course the Nieces, including me. The proof records of Menuhin's performance of the Concerto had only just arrived, delighting E. E. so much that he longed for all to share his joy and amazement at the youth's deep insight into what often seemed to him to be his most inspired work. After the recording of it he had written:

I do not think there is anything <u>quite </u>like it, and some day perhaps it will be understood how much soul went into the making of it: the soloist is a marvel, and got more and more into it and more and more out of it as we went on, don't you think? I began to like the Concerto myself.

So here we all sat, spellbound at the glorious sounds, G. B. S. with bowed head, sometimes softly singing with the music; Aircraftman Shaw serious and silent, looking straight ahead with those unforgettable blue eyes which seemed to see into the life of things. After Menuhin had lovingly lingered over the last melting phrases of the Slow Movement, E. E. whispered "This is where two souls merge and melt into one another."

Many would consider it sacrilege to attempt to find words to accompany such unearthly music, which must remain on that rarified plane where the sublime works of art seem to meet and blend themselves into the Eternal Mind, The Eternal Truth. Yet I feel I almost have E. E.'s authority for quoting Shelley's "Epipsychidion."

Epipsychidion, *whose title is thought to mean something like 'soul out of my soul,' represents a search for the poet's spiritual mate, and was evidently another work by Shelley which interested Elgar and which he shared with Vera. It was an autobiographical poem that Shelley had written at Pisa in 1821 as a result of repeated visits to Teresa Viviani, a beautiful and intelligent seventeen year-old heiress strictly confined by her family to a nunnery until a suitable husband could be chosen for her. Through an account of his Platonic love for the young girl, Shelley recapitulated his search for ideal Beauty and Love, the 'eternal feminine,' sometimes defining, as Elgar did, a single archetypal figure combining several rôles. And if Shelley's search for an essential female presence, like Elgar's, was lifelong, the passage that Vera quotes from the final section of the poem, an imaginary voyage with the beloved to an island paradise, might amount to a Liebestod.*

> We shall become the same, we shall be one
> Spirit within two frames, oh wherefore two?
>
> In one anothers substance finding food
> Like flames too pure and light and unimbued
> To nourish their bright lives with baser prey
> One hope within two wills, one will beneath
> Two overshadowing minds, one life, one death,
> One Heaven, one Hell, one immortality,
> And one annihilation.

This memorable Three Choirs Meeting of 1932 was to be Elgar's last appearance at a Worcester Festival, and he must undoubtedly have had a premonition that this was so, for as I was reluctantly leaving Marl Bank I was presented with a Novello's vocal and piano score of the "Music Makers" and upon opening it I found underlined the very last line of the poem:

> "A singer who sings no more.
>   i.e. Edward Elgar."

*

It was another of the messages that signified Elgar's own uncertainty over his ability to resume large-scale composition successfully. But in the heady atmosphere of that sunny Festival week in his own beloved city, where he had conducted some of his greatest works, and had been at the centre of a circle of admiring friends, including of course Vera, events seemed to take control. A remark Elgar made about the Third Symphony at a tea party was taken up in a report in the *Daily Mail*, assuming that the work was completed and demanding that it be performed. The matter was now fully in the public domain and the momentum continued to gather when at the end of the month Shaw wrote persuasively to Sir John Reith to suggest that the BBC could 'bring the Third Symphony into existence and obtain the performing right for the BBC for, say, ten years, for a few thousand pounds.' Shaw knew his man and emphasized the prestige such a commission would bring to the BBC, likening it to the London Philharmonic Society's dealings with Beethoven over the Ninth Symphony. He pressed home the attack by saying that he knew that Elgar had 'the material for the first movement ready, because he has played it to me on his piano.' And he implied that Elgar was unable to devote himself to the composition of a symphony because it would mean turning aside from more lucrative, if unspecified, work; ' . . . he has still a lot of stuff in him that could be released if he could sit down to it without risking his livelihood.' The main burden of the letter was, in fact, financial. 'Everybody seems to assume either that Elgar can live on air, or that he is so rich and successful that he can afford to write symphonies and conduct festivals for nothing. As a matter of fact his financial position is a very difficult one . . .' And with the skilled help of Sir Landon Ronald as negotiator, a contract was drawn up between Elgar and the BBC for the Third Symphony, and signed early in December. Under its terms he was to receive the sum of £250 a quarter payable in arrear 'during such time as the composer may be engaged upon the proposed musical work or for a period of one year whichever is the shorter,' together with a separate payment of £1, 000 on completion of the work. This fee on completion was of course exactly the sum Elgar owed Bernard Shaw. But Elgar was still not entirely confident. In writing to thank Reith, he concluded by saying that 'whatever happens' he would always treasure the remembrance of his 'kindness & consideration,' and earlier he had written to Basil Maine, 'I fear there is nothing to say in regard to the new Symphony or anything else: things take shape without my knowing it – I am only the lead pencil and cannot foresee.'

Meanwhile, one Sunday early in October, Carice recorded a day trip to Robin Hill; it would have been immediately after a 'mensiversary:'

Sunday 9 October, 1932. To Church at 9. left at 10. 30 for Vera's – got there at 12. 15. Father & she arrived just after. Nice time. Father rested after lunch & we had to leave at 4 so did not see him much. Home before 6.

As the year drew to its close Elgar was kept busy with various conducting engagements, including broadcast performances of *Gerontius* and *King Olaf*. More notably he directed Menuhin in a performance of the Violin Concerto at the Albert Hall, or 'Bert' as the Elgars disparagingly named it, and shortly afterwards the BBC Symphony Orchestra gave a series of three special concerts to mark his 75th birthday. Carice attended each of these events, leaving her becolded husband behind. She stayed with Vera in Croydon as before, travelling with her up to town for rehearsals, concerts and meals at the Langham. The Violin Concerto performance took place on the afternoon of Sunday, 20th November. By now Vera had a car of her own, and Carice began to use a word that would often reappear in her diary when writing of the time they spent together: 'lovely.'

Saturday 19 November. Busy am. Left for Vera about 11 – took Sam to Petworth cold coming on – Lovely quiet afternoon & evening with Vera. Records etc.

Sunday 20 November. Vera & I left in my car about 9 & got to Albert Hall by 9. 45. Met Father & Col Isaac & heard all rehearsal – wonderful.

Lunched with Father at Langham & took taxi back to Bert – marvellous audience, concert & everything – To Mrs. Marks to tea & back to Langham – Drove Father & Vera down about 7. Lovely evening.

Monday 21 November. Vera & I in car (hired) to Langham with Father in am. She took me out in hers after & we had a walk. Left after lunch – home about tea time. Sam coldy.

The first of the three birthday concerts, in which Elgar conducted *Cockaigne* and the Violin Concerto, this time with Albert Sammons, coincided with domestic distractions. Again it was a hectic time for Carice, but there was time for a walking interlude with Vera's spaniel, Pan Yan Pickle:

Wednesday 30 November. Men down to see to boiler – new one needed. Sam to Chichester. Left about 11 & got to Vera for lunch. Father rang up. All right. Vera & I with Pan. Went to E. Croydon in my car on by train & taxi. Dined with Father at Langham – & concert. Wonderful evening – huge reception – Went to Hotel after & home same way –

Thursday 1 December. Nice am. Vera & I in her car shopping. Left after early lunch & went to W. I. Committee. Home by 4 took dogs out. Sam to sale of poultry at Rogate – did not buy any there but ordered some from a man he saw. Father home in am.

At the second concert on 7th December, Elgar conducted the *Enigma* Variations and the Second Symphony. The evening before, he played his sketches for the Opera for Vera and Carice at Robin Hill.

Tuesday 6 December. Decided to go to London. Sam uncertain – left about 11. Lunch with Vera & went up to fetch Father – called on Miss Norris in Brixton. Robin Hill to tea. Nice evening. Seeing opera MSS & hearing it etc.

Wednesday 7 December. Lovely sun – hard frost. Went to London with Father about 10 – Vera & I to rehearsal – 2nd Symphony. Went to the Davidsons to lunch – Vera home – came & fetched me in her car. Back to Robin Hill to tea. Up to concert via E. Croydon – Wonderful evening.

Thursday 8 December. Very cold wind – Father home by 9. 45. Vera & I walk with Pan Jan. Left after lunch – Home by 4. 0. Took dogs – No hot water – boiler being done –

That day the arrangements for the Third Symphony were ready to go through the BBC's legal department and the publisher. ' . . . the Elgar business is finally fixed up,' noted Reith in his diary. 'Ronald lunched with me today. Jardine Brown can now put the thing through with Keith Prowse and Elgar.' The final birthday concert, with Boult conducting *The Kingdom*, closely coincided with a performance of the Variations given at Croydon by Billy Reed's orchestra. On the evening of the *Kingdom* performance, Landon Ronald publicly announced the Third Symphony commission at a Guildhall dinner.

Tuesday 13 December. Very foggy early. Cleared about midday – went to Petworth – & immediately after lunch drove to Vera – no fog. Went to Mr. Reed's Concert at W. Croydon – Variations. Sat with Mrs. Reed – & met Croydon people. Round with them to their house after, nice time. Father came to London.

Wednesday 14 December. Sam to Chichester. Drove Vera up to Langham – & went to rehearsal of Kingdom. Lunched with Father. Back to Robin Hill & came to dine with Father & to concert. B. B. C. announcement of producing III Symphony made. Father came back to Robin Hill after concert – Sat talking till 1 a.m.

Thursday 15 December. Father to London about 10 – drove up with him & back to Shirley Park Hotel – walked thro Park back to Robin Hill. Left directly after lunch home by 4. Had vet up again to fetch bones.

So clearly Vera, no less than Carice, had been a quietly supportive presence throughout the whole heady period. The adulation Elgar received during the birthday concerts had been intense, and the announcement of the commissioning of the symphony was greeted with excited acclaim by press and public. Shaw wrote a letter to *The Times* lauding Reith as 'a public administrator capable of rising to the situation,' and acclaiming the commission as 'a triumph for the BBC.' Landon Ronald produced a celebratory article praising Elgar's creative powers and making sure that the BBC received its due measure of thanks:

There have been many instances of great men producing masterpieces in comparative old age. Musically, I need only quote such famous examples as Verdi's 'Falstaff' written at the age of 80, and 'Parsifal,' which was only completed in Wagner's 70th year. Elgar is in no sense an old man. His creative powers are as great as ever and he is as vigorous and as alert as the ordinary man of 50. Judging by the way the public acclaimed him at the recent Elgar Celebration Concerts, there can be no possible doubt that his music has gone to the hearts of the people. And now we shall await his latest work with wonder and belief; and our gratitude goes out to the BBC for an action which can be best described by the word which Elgar uses so often as a mark of expression in his scores: NOBILMENTE.'

But Ronald's expectations were dauntingly high. He wrote: 'It is my belief that he may give us not only a masterpiece – I take that for granted – but that he may write something even more mature and more inspired than any thing we have yet heard from him.' The burden of such expectations led Elgar to further self-deprecatory outbursts to Vera, who remembered meeting him one evening as she was on her way with Dulcie to enjoy a performance of *Gerontius*. 'You poor things,' said the composer, 'an evening of Gerry's Nightmare! I am going to the Windmill.'

A former friend and confidante, Rosa Burley, headmistress of the Malvern school at which Carice had been a boarder, unexpectedly received a Christmas card from Elgar that year, and offered an explanation which with the benefit of hindsight seems astute enough:

> At the Christmas of 1932 . . . I was surprised to receive a card from him. It had been posted in the Earl's Court district and was inscribed simply, 'From Edward.' As he had resolutely cut me for many years and as even our years of friendship had brought me a good deal of pain, I was careful in writing a letter of thanks to indicate as gently as possible that I did not wish to resume our past relationship. But I was puzzled by this sudden mark of recognition and wondered why it had been made. Could it be that he hoped by reviving an old friendship to recapture some of the youthful urge towards composition of past years? I shall never know.

And in the wake of the symphony announcement there came another reminder of a friend from days past, this time of his most intimate artistic advisor, whose uniquely perceptive criticism had helped to mould the final form of Elgar's first masterpieces, the *Enigma* Variations and *Gerontius*, August Jaeger. Jaeger had been dead and almost forgotten these twenty-three years, but his widow now sought an opportunity to keep his name and influence alive. On 17th December the 'London Day by Day' column of the *Daily Telegraph* carried this paragraph:

> The fact that Sir Edward Elgar is engaged upon the composition of another symphony is properly acclaimed in the world of music as an event of the first magnitude. Sir Edward has been a long time coming into his own with the English public, who find it hard to believe in the ecumenical greatness of the native-born musician. But for his friend, A. J. Jaeger, he might have had to wait much longer for recognition. Jaeger was one of Novello's readers, and by his persistency he forced his employers to give ear to his

protege. It is also said that he influenced the form of some part at least of Elgar's music. The "Enigma Variations," in particular – the work which brought Elgar into notice – owes, I am told, a good deal of its popular appeal to Jaeger's flair. Elgar was a constant visitor to the Jaeger household at Muswell-hill thirty years ago, and his music frequently floated over the garden fences to ears which little suspected the eminence of its source.

And at the family Christmas dinner, Elgar appeared suitably cheerful about the work. 'Now if you'll all blow on your whistles, I'll put the sound into my new Symphony,' he said after the crackers had been opened. And at the new year he sent Vera his first sketches for the opening of the first movement, with a brief, backdated message that showed how close she was to him and the music; 'First thought for Sym III and last thought for V. H. Jany. 1933 E. E. Or rather, 31st Decr 1932.'

*

The beloved must have her *idée fixe*. There was another, undated, page of sketches that he sent to her, too, including ten bars of the second subject of the first movement – Vera's music. This time the inscription was '1st Sketch of VH's own theme above. Will never be finished?' Elgar's pessimism over the completion of the entire work was justified, as we know, but he was able to complete another sketch using Vera's music in another context. It was marked 'near the end' and featured her feminine melody punctuating the first movement's opening, masculine music every two bars, as if the two elements were in dialogue, the one seeming to calm the other. Or perhaps it was another moment when two souls could merge and melt into one another.

With the first performance planned for the autumn, Elgar laid the opera aside at the beginning of 1933 in order to focus as best he could on the symphony, with Billy Reed visiting and playing through the sketches with him. But Reed could not get beyond the sense of a collection of fragments, with much material taken from earlier sketches and even the opera being raided, and Elgar continued openly uneasy about the work. In February the first instalment of £250 arrived from the BBC, and Reith noted on his copy of the accompanying letter, 'cheque drawn 23/2/33.' It was a year to the very day before the composer's death. Signs of the onset of his final illness, in addition to the 'sciatica' and 'lumbago' that he had been experiencing for some time, were not long in coming. Towards the end of April he suffered a mysterious, if brief, seizure and at this time, in response to a degree of pressure from the BBC, anxious to have the maximum advance notice of the work for publicity purposes, it was agreed that the première would be put back to the spring of 1934. But within a few days of his illness, Elgar was able to play Carice some opera and symphony sketches and Wulstan Atkins remembered hearing some of the symphony during a visit to Marl Bank at the end of the month.

However, what he heard were fragments in no particular order. Elgar seemed active and vital despite a tendency to tire easily, and it is tempting to see Vera's continuing effect on the composer in Atkins's description of him at this time:

> During the first half of 1933 he showed a restless activity, and judging from his conversation life seemed for him to be coloured in vivid hues, no longer in the soft pastel shades of nostalgia. There was a vividness in whatever he did. When one was with him one could feel the 'hum' as it were of a great dynamo. I mentioned this to my father and he said that I was letting my imagination run away with me, but he did agree that Elgar was now mentally in the state in which he remembered him in the days of his greatest creativity.

That year Carice and Vera further developed their friendship. They visited each other, Vera coming to Petworth and staying for a night in January. 'Nice time with her,' wrote Carice, who however was 'worried re Sam,' who had had to take to his bed with a 'bad head.' By the time of Vera's next visit, early in March, he was better although an early night was necessary. Vera had originally planned to come just for the afternoon, but she 'rang up car broken down so fetched her from Petworth & had her for night. Lovely time.' And at the end of the month there was an opportunity for a general get-together at Robin Hill, with a sentimental journey to the Crystal Palace and a theatre in the evening.

> Thursday 30 March 1933. Had my hair done 10. 15. Miss Payne & on to Vera for lunch. Walk for Panny. Some showers. Went up to London & Dulcie by 6. She & Vera home. Met Father. Went to AGM dinner. Very nice. Sir G Bantock, D. Tovey and Mr Woods there. Vera fetched us from Langham & went to Robin Hill – talking till late.

> Friday 31 March 1933. Lovely am. Father down early in garden. Left about 11 & went to Crystal Palace on way up – met the manager & Father asked for old programmes. Enjoyed seeing statues & concert hall. On to Langham. Vera & I back, quiet afternoon. Went to Langham to dinner – met Steuart Wilson – & on to Once in a Lifetime again.

Vera 'left early for her rehearsal' the next morning, but the two women met up again in April when ' Vera came early after lunch & stayed till 7. Lovely to have her.'

May saw another few days at Croydon to rehearse and conduct Alan Kirby's Croydon Philharmonic Society in a performance of *The Apostles*. Vera and Billy Reed and his wife James provided their usual hospitality, and there was a visit from Landon Ronald. The chorus made Elgar a special presentation, and welcome diversions such as tadpoles and horseracing were enjoyed; but it proved to be the last time that he would conduct the work.

Friday 5 May. Busy am. Miss Payne at 2 oc & on to Croydon by 4. 30. Vera & I to tea – & went to dine at Reeds. Father there rather tired after his journey. Choral rehearsal – wonderful chorus presented him with green and white clock. To Reeds on way home.

Saturday 6 May. Billy brought Father over in am. He & I in car to get fishing net & got tadpoles from pond below Vera's. To lunch at Reeds & on to full rehearsal – wonderful – tea at Reed's – Harold Brooke there. Vera met Miss Desmond over to fetch her luggage from Hall – Crowded streets & rain. Back to Robin Hill & to dinner here – there – To Concert – wonderful performance & reception. To Reeds afterwards.

Sunday 7 May. Wet early but cleared more or less later. To church in Lower Addiscombe Road at 10. Billy & James brought Father over about 12. 30 – & lunched – left after trying III Symphony on violin. Landon Ronalds to tea. Quiet evening. Father playing Symphony Apostles etc.

Monday 8 May. Took Father to Reeds early – & he & Dick left for Newmarket – Vera & I put them in right road. Back to Robin Hill – left soon after. Home by 1. 30. Sam Barnham. Getting ready for sweep. In drawing room for evening.

Less than three weeks later there was another foregathering when Elgar flew from Croydon airport to Paris to conduct another performance of the Violin Concerto with Yehudi Menuhin as soloist. There was time for the composer to spend some happy hours with the whole Menuhin family, where he nominated himself an honorary grandfather to the children, and to make his celebrated visit to Delius at Grez-sur-Loing. Greatly to his disappointment, Eric Fenby missed meeting Elgar again on this occasion, as he had had to travel urgently to London to go through some proofs at Boosey & Hawkes. He wrote his regrets and used the opportunity to assure the composer how greatly he was looking forward to the production of the new symphony. Despite another 'bad turn' the day before the journey, the whole remarkable undertaking – the flight itself, the concert, and his friendly, animated conversations with Delius, a man with whom Elgar had not previously had a particularly successful relationship – was another example of a continuing capacity for enjoying life, a healthy enough sign for a man on the verge of his seventy-sixth birthday. 'Delius is a man with a future,' wrote Elgar in his account of the meeting, and perhaps he now felt the same about himself. Vera assisted at both departure and return:

Saturday 27 May 1933. Went to E Croydon to be there to meet Father. Went with Vera to Reeds about 3. 30. He came about 4 – very heavy showers. Went to Robin Hill for dinner where he stayed. Vera took Mrs Reed home later. Father had had another bad turn but seemed quite all right again.

Sunday 28 May 1933. Went to Church at 8. Lovely quiet am at Robin Hill – puzzle etc. Went to Mrs Reeds for lunch. I drove Father & Vera's car came too for luggage. Saw him from aerodrome – wonderful to see it – photographers etc & great excitement. Lovely weather. Got home about 7. 30. Were all well.

Elgar returned to Croydon on the following Friday, his birthday. Carice drove up early from Petworth and joined with Vera to meet him. Meanwhile Shaw, who had learnt of the Paris trip, kept up the pressure. 'How does the symphony get on?' he wrote. 'Dont you think you could get two into the time? Remember, you have to catch up on Beethoven.'

Friday 2 June 1933. Sheep shearers came. Lovely day. left at 8. 30 & got to Vera's at 10.15 went on with her to Aerodrome. Plane half an hour early so could not see it land. Father all safe & very well & had loved it – Mr Gaisberg too. Drove him to Mr Reed's had champagne for his birthday & heard about Paris & Delius. Mr Gaisberg & photographers came & took pictures of him being toasted. He left with Dick for Worcester about 12. 30. Vera & I to see lovely spaniel puppy & back to lunch & sat out after looking at birds. Early tea & left about 3. 45, shopping at Dorking & home about 6. 30. Very hot.

Vera seems to have kept well out of the various photographs that were taken on that occasion, possibly quite deliberately as at some stage she had been gently warned that her relationship with Elgar was beginning to be a source of comment. The following Thursday she drove down to Petworth for an afternoon with Carice – 'lunch & long walk by river . . . lovely time,' and the two women met up again later in the month at Marl Bank: 'Vera rang up she was at Malvern so fetched her . . . to tea & dinner & took her back later.' The next day they met at Pershore and drove on to Woodstock for lunch, although Vera's next appearance in Carice's diary was not until mid-August, when she ' wrote Dulcie was laid up at Keswick.'
That summer proved uncomfortably hot, not perhaps conducive to the sustained labour of composition and scoring, and once the excitement of the Paris trip was over, Elgar felt drained and unwell, suggesting to Billy Reed at the end of June that there was no need for him to come and play any more sketches. But the flame continued to flicker. A month later they played some symphony for the Shaws, and a few days after that Elgar summoned Basil Maine to hear a piano

rendition of the music as far as it went, although Maine came away with the impression that he had heard much more music than was actually written down in the sketches. Fred Gaisberg also heard a good deal of the work that summer. All were impressed, but the symphony hung by a thread. The composer seemed to lack the vital urge to forge ahead and clinch the whole thing and Maine wrote of the 'moody restlessness' which the work seemed to induce in him. During that August Elgar's secretary Mary Clifford thought that he had in fact begun to neglect the symphony in favour of the opera. The perceptive Gaisberg thought 'some sympathetic person, lady or man, of strong character should take him in hand and drive him on. Some exciter is needed to inflame him.' Vera's presence was not continuous and she would in any case be the last person able to emulate Alice's occasionally quite ruthless determination to make Elgar work. Behind it all, his illness was quietly taking its toll and would shortly move to a crisis. When he appeared at a Queen's Hall Promenade concert to conduct the Second Symphony for the last time on 17th August, Elgar was visibly unwell, shrunken and trembling, and he sat to conduct. Carice went round to the Langham afterwards '& talked to Father in bed.'

A fortnight later Carice stayed with Vera for a few days while her father directed a recording session at Kingsway Hall followed by a Three Choirs rehearsal. Vera attended the latter and as if to mark the occasion, took both her children. 'Vera & Dulcie & John & I up in her car for rehearsal,' noted Carice, who wrote later that she felt sure throughout the summer that they were doing things for the last time. At the Hereford Festival which immediately followed, much of the burden of the day-to-day arrangements would have fallen on her shoulders, on top of her anxieties about her father's health. A house with a large garden was taken for the week, and it seemed to be a success: 'Father went with Mary to Hereford . . . House seemed to settle down quickly – Father liked it.' Billy Reed noted that Elgar did not want to move about very much or go for walks, but his customary Festival hospitality continued and a succession of friends and visitors were entertained in the garden throughout the week. Wulstan Atkins noted how quickly the composer tired and how he always used a walking-stick; he noticed, too, how, unusually, Elgar seemed to want to talk about music. Basil Maine particularly remembered a conversation in the garden between Elgar and Bernard Shaw after the Tuesday performance of *Elijah* when, in response to Shaw's criticism of Mendelssohn's orchestration, Elgar produced the full score and demonstrated much evidence to the contrary. Several photographs were taken of the two men that afternoon, and they very much give us the dynamics of the conversation. More than that, they suggest the continuing importance for him of Vera's proximity to the composer; in one photograph she is seen sitting on the lawn somewhat behind his chair, a relaxed, taken-for-granted supportive presence with an affectionate arm around a friend who had joined her for the Festival. They would see him conduct memorable performances of *Gerontius*, the Cello

Concerto in Tertis's arrangement for viola, and, on the Thursday morning, *The Kingdom* – the last time he would conduct. Perhaps people suspected this, and no doubt Vera had her own intuitions about Elgar's condition, just as Carice did.

Towards the end of September, Carice had 'Vera & Dulcie to tea' at Petworth, but shortly afterwards her diary entries peter out and it would be more than two years before she would have time or inclination to continue them. Her father became ill at the beginning of October and was taken to the South Bank nursing home in Worcester, undergoing an exploratory operation which revealed inoperable cancer. Intuitively knowing the worst, Elgar informed Reith of the situation and its implications for the symphony, and mentioned the arrangements he had made for the return of the monies that had been paid. Reith replied kindly but was evidently not willing to relinquish all prospect of the Symphony. The BBC sent representatives to encourage the composer to allow an operation to cut the spinal cord, relieving him of pain and allowing him to continue composing the work, although it was not clear how the actual scoring might be achieved in such circumstances. In this respect Eric Fenby made his own independent approach, offering to act as amanuensis for Elgar, just as he had for Delius. Billy Reed did the same. But all such overtures were decisively rejected and he told one of his doctors, 'If I can't complete the Third Symphony, somebody else will complete it – or write a better one – in fifty or five hundred years. Viewed from the point where I am now, on the brink of eternity, that's a mere moment in time.' Later he would change his mind over a completion of the symphony, for after a serious relapse towards the end of November he haltingly asked Billy Reed that no-one should tinker with it, and even that it should be burnt. Reed, in the presence of Carice, was at any rate able to promise that ' no one would ever tamper with it in any way.' He could do no less.

From that low point Elgar made something of an unexpected, if temporary, recovery. He asked to be photographed and was able to enjoy music on a gramophone that was set up for him. He dictated letters and received visitors including Ernest Newman, Landon Ronald, Ivor Atkins, Basil Maine and Mary Anderson. The symphony continued to be on his mind and he wrote out brief extracts for Reed and Newman. At the beginning of January 1934 it was decided that he could return to Marl Bank to be cared for, and later that month he was able to direct by land line the historic recording of excerpts from *Caractacus* by the London Symphony Orchestra. But there could be no escape from the inevitable. Heavily drugged as he was to dull his pain, Elgar continually drifted in and out of dream-laden periods of unconsciousness. 'He is greatly living in the most extraordinary dreams,' Carice told Ernest Newman. Billy Reed described what he saw of the process of negation and collapse, but against all hope:

> I began to see visions of his ultimate recovery; and, though I anticipated
> that he would always be an invalid, I thought it just possible that he would

be able to take up the threads of his Third Symphony after all, and even muster enough health and strength to finish it. But this was not to be. In his own home he slowly but surely slipped downhill. I went there constantly from London, and it was pitiful to see him receding, fading away from us all so certainly that there was no doubt about the hopelessness of his illness. The only wonder was that he fought so long and so patiently before he left us finally on February 23rd, 1934.

After their meeting at Marl Bank to listen to the Violin Concerto, a brief correspondence had developed between Elgar and T. E. Lawrence, who wrote of repeated playings of the Second Symphony at Clouds Hill and of his eagerness to hear the new symphony. And to Charlotte Shaw he confessed that no other composer 'gets so inside my defences as he does.' Now he wrote Carice a letter of condolence in which he wrote of the happiness her father's music had given him and affirming the Shaws' affection for the composer. 'And no 3rd. Symphony after all,' he concluded. 'It is a tragedy.' It was nothing less than the truth.

*

And amidst all such traffic of the great and good, what of Vera all this time, and her thoughts for her dying Hyperion, and his for one who was his guardian, child, lover, and friend? What passed between them? Did she visit him and was he able to write to her? What farewells did they make? We can only speculate, for no documentary record exists to satisfy our curiosity. Carice seems not to have kept a diary at this time and all Elgar's letters to Vera would be destroyed after her death. Others who might have known judged it best to keep silence. Vera was not recorded as being present at the funeral, or at the memorial service that was held in Worcester Cathedral at the beginning of March. But more truly than many people who had known Edward Elgar, she had much to treasure in her heart.

'Love to Vera from Billy'

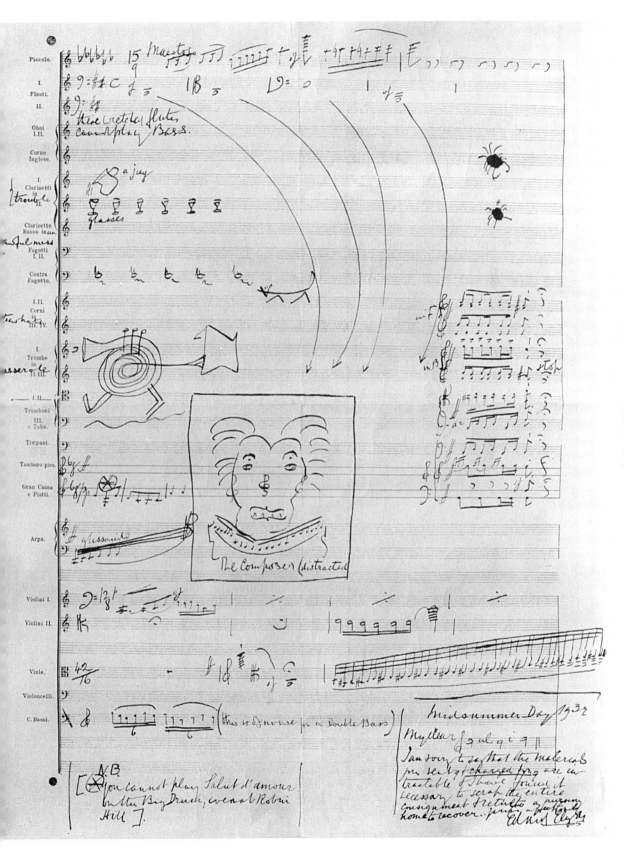

Dulcie's joke score

Elgar at the Hereford Festival, 1933

Elgar arriving at the cathedral, Worcester Festival 1932

'Will never be finished?' Two pages of Third Symphony sketches

given to Vera, including the '1st sketch of V.H.'s own theme.'

Elgar with the Menuhin family in Paris, 30th May, 1933

Vera and friend at the Hereford Festival, 1933 with Elgar and Shaw

Elgar in conversation with the Shaws, Worcester Festival 1932

GBS and Charlotte, Gloucester Festival 1934

Carice and motor car. A friend recalled of their outings, 'I was always frightened out of my wits because she was a rotten driver.'

Southampton

24. 2. 34

Dear Mrs Blake

A useless, silly letter of which you must take
no notice ; but his music has made me so often happy
that his going becomes a personal loss — unreasonable
when I only met him once. I am so sorry.

G.B.S. and Mrs Shaw liked him properly, out
of full knowledge. They are at sea, but will radio you
something, I expect. You would have liked to ~~see~~ overhear
as I did, how real their admiration and affection was.

And no 3rd Symphony after all. It is tragedy.

Yours,
TEShaw

A letter of condolence from Lawrence of Arabia

Billy Reed conducting the brass chorales from the cathedral tower, Worcester Festival 1938

Ivor and Wulstan Atkins, Worcester Festival 1935

Chapter 3 Life Goes On.

A miscellany of surviving documents enables us to trace some aspects of the fate of the Third Symphony – about which Bernard Shaw had not spoken his last – and of the lives of Carice and Vera, whose admiration of 'Uncle Ralph' led her to keep his letters.

Some few days before Elgar's death, too late for a reply, Vaughan Williams had written to the composer asking for his blessing on a performance of *The Dream of Gerontius* that he was to conduct in April as part of the Leith Hill Festival. It would be the first time that the sixty-two year old composer conducted the work which had influenced him so much in the early years of the century, and he told Elgar '. . . it will be one of the great moments of my life when I stand with trembling baton to conduct it.' Inevitably the performance, the first complete one since the composer's death, took on something of the nature of a requiem. Vera played in the orchestra, and Carice was in the audience, with what feelings we can only imagine. Vera wrote immediately afterwards to the conductor, who replied

The White Gates,
Westcott Road,
Dorking.

[April 1934]

Dear Vera,
   How wonderful and sweet of you to write at once. I love having all you dear people round me making music with such devotion to the art – it is a great experience for me. I wanted to embrace you all, but the occasion was too public. Mrs Blake was so wonderfully sympathetic.
   We must carry out our plan one Wednesday early in June.

Love from Uncle Ralph.

P. S. Do you think Mrs Blake would write me a line to pass on to the choirs?

Although the responsibility of her father's illness and death was over, Carice was beginning to embark on another, lifelong, burden, that of a sort of official Elgarian spokesperson. Vera passed the message on and Carice duly obliged: '. . . I do want you to know what a wonderful performance I thought it,' she wrote to V.W., '& to thank you for all the love & care & the tremendous amount of work you put into it. The choir sang marvellously, & the whole atmosphere was so beautiful & what my father would have loved I feel.'

Vera shared her love of poetry with Vaughan Williams just as she had with Elgar and that July sent him some words for setting. The composer responded with thanks and news of a temporary incapacity. He had embarked on a walk to the coast after Gustav Holst's funeral service at Chichester Cathedral in June and cut his foot while bathing. The wound became poisoned and he was confined to bed for eight weeks.

The White Gates,
Westcott Road,
Dorking.

Sunday [July 1934]

My Dearest Vera,
How very sweet of you to send me the Poetry book – many of the poems I know & love but many are new to me & I have already marked some for future use.
Wasn't it silly of me – I went for a long walk & then neglected a blister & so got a poisoned leg. I am still in bed & not allowed to move it though I feel perfectly well.
I shall not soon forget our lovely romantic evening at Robin Hill. How lovely that you are to be at Gloucester.

Love from Uncle Ralph

Vera held frequent 'musical evenings' in her beautiful house. The problem with the leg continued so severe that Vaughan Williams was unable to attend that year's Three Choirs Festival, the first since Elgar's death, but Vera would have heard the Second Symphony, *The Kingdom*, and a memorable performance of *The Dream of Gerontius* conducted by Ivor Atkins. Wulstan remembered clearly how 'unashamed tears rolled down many cheeks that evening.' Billy Reed led the orchestra and GBS would have been present, and there may have been some discussion between them about the Elgar book that Reed would publish two years later with Shaw's advice and encouragement. There certainly seems to have been some conversation between the two men over the question of the completion of the Third Symphony from the sketch material that Reed and Carice had saved from the flames, for a letter of August 1934 suggests that Reed had made a direct appeal to Shaw for his opinion. His reply seems to indicate that the matter had been approached in musicological rather than ethical terms, as if he had been asked if he thought it might be technically feasible for the Symphony to be completed by another hand; Granville Bantock, for one, offered his services. Shaw replied that while what he referred to as the 'clear symmetrical patterns' of the music of such composers as Haydn and Rossini might lend themselves to completion by another hand, the freer forms established later by the Romantics meant that such reconstruction was impossible:

> What is a symphony? A hundred years ago it was a composition in a clear symmetrical pattern established by Haydn and called Sonata Form. Now if half a symmetrical design is completed, any draughtsman can supply the missing half. If Haydn had died during the composition of one of his symphonies, and had left notes of its themes, and a hint or two of its bridge passages, Beethoven could easily have contributed a perfect Haydn symphony from them as an act of piety ot a musical *jeu d'esprit.*
>
> On the same terms any educated musician could construct an unfinished Rossini overture.
>
> But no composer of symphonies nowadays adheres to the decorative patterns. The musical romances and extravaganzas of Berlioz, the symphonic poems of Liszt and Strauss, and the tone-dramas of Wagner could not have conformed to symmetrical decorative patterns: they had to find expressionist forms; and to reconstruct a lost expressionist composition from a fragment would be as impossible as to reconstruct a Shakespeare sonnet from the first two lines of it.
>
> All the great symphonies after Beethoven are as expressionist as Wagner's music-dramas, even when, as in the Symphonies of Brahms and Elgar, the skeleton of the old pattern is still discernible. All possibility of reconstruction from fragments or completion from beginnings is gone.
>
> Consequently, though Elgar left some sketches of a third symphony and was actually at work on it when he died, no completion or reconstruction is possible: the symphony, like Beethoven's tenth, died with the composer.

Shaw's tone was dogmatic, but modern musicology and Haydn scholarship would, I imagine, completely dismiss his ideas about Haydn, and Tony Payne has triumphantly kept the Elgar symphony alive.

*

The January 1935 issue of *Music & Letters* was given over to Elgarian tributes, including an article by Vaughan Williams, 'What have we learnt from Elgar?' It contained praise of the composer's orchestral and choral writing and of the way he had achieved a 'bond of unity' with his countrymen. With characteristic humility V.W. went on to describe how deeply Elgar's music had influenced the development of his style, even to the direct 'cribbing' of a phrase from *Gerontius*. He discussed the development of Elgar's music and stimulatingly suggested that the 'small and rather charming' music of such organists as Henry Smart and John Goss would have been an early influence. But in doing so he immediately felt it necessary to defend himself against the expected protests of 'distinguished artists and literary men who know nothing and care less about the subject' followed by the 'vapourings' of Shaw. And there was further mauling of Shaw when V.W. recounted the help that Elgar had undoubtedly received around the turn of the century from the 'great men' who 'certain journalists . . . are pleased to call "academics," because they happened to be learned as well as musical,' namely Parry and Stanford. There had grown up a myth that they had completely cold-shouldered Elgar, a 'false scent' that had been started by Shaw 'with characteristic disregard of facts' and which received a 'well-deserved snub' from Elgar himself. Shaw was hurt, although he seems not to have sought any opportunity for a public riposte. Privately he wrote to Troyte Griffith, 'I was surprised at V. W. suddenly sticking his knife into me; I must take some opportunity of conciliating him; for he has no reason to class me with litterateurs who write on music without knowing anything about it.' Shaw admitted looking Vaughan Williams up in *Grove's Dictionary* only to find that he was a 'survivor' of the 'university clique' himself but he was prepared to allow that the composer's contribution to the *Music & Letters* collection was one of the few with 'anything real' in it. However the article seems not to have met with a favourable reception generally, although there was one friend of both writer and subject who took the trouble to praise it:

The White Gates,
Westcott Road,
Dorking.

[Jan] 27th [1935]

Dearest Vera,

I hope this will catch you before you flit from your Robins Nest. Thankyou so much for your letter – the only one which has said anything nice about my article. I am so glad you liked it. It was not meant to be more than a few stray ideas.

Love from

RVW

The Robin's Nest was the title of Vaughan Williams's first composition, a four-bar piano piece written at the age of six.

*

That April of 1935 Vera met the man who was to be her partner for the rest of her life. The new relationship developed quickly, and she felt impelled to document its first few few weeks, just as she had with *The Story of November 7th.* This time her writing was more brief and fragmentary, but it is still possible to gain from it a vivid sense of Vera's feelings and experience. As if to underline the special intimacy of the new relationship, she used some spare sheets of Elgar's blue Florentine notepaper for her writing, essentially a list of lovers' meetings with dates; it was headed *The First Spring* and prefaced by a quotation, 'So sweet love seemed that April morn . . .'

His name was Charles Henry Cheeseman, and once again music was the point of contact, for he was then a freelance double-bass player who had gained a scholarship to the Royal College of Music as a student. For a time, in order to supplement an uncertain income, he also ran a record and concert-ticket business, The Tudor Shop, at Kew. Playing in the cinemas before the days of talking films, his resemblance to a screen Don Giovanni led colleagues to dub him Don, and the name stuck. During the Second World War he taught at the Kneller Hall Military School of Music, and subsequently he was chosen by Beecham to be one of the original members of the Royal Philharmonic Orchestra, playing with it from its inception. Don was, however, modest about his proficiency as a player, a proficiency he maintained by hard work – regularly retiring with his Amati instrument to a sanctuary in the garden to practise – in contrast with Vera's more intuitive, easy-going musicianship.

Perhaps the pair had previously encountered each other at rehearsals from time to time, but Vera began by noting a meeting on 11th April, a rehearsal at a church hall, followed by 'tea at confectioners.' 'It seems we are fated to meet, & then lose sight of one another,' she added. But no longer. There was another rehearsal the next day, followed by tea and sherry 'then drive to Landport in moonlit twilight.' After a further rehearsal Vera recorded a 'letter given at tea at The Crown. No shadow of doubt. Delirious joy.' On 15th April she returned to Robin Hill, to receive a first letter and phone call, and on 17th Don paid his first visit to the lovely house in the Shirley pine woods. 'Showers of presents cause much merriment,' wrote Vera, but there were serious matters to be dealt with as well: 'Discuss his marriage at 23 and the war experiences until the small hours. Less & less doubt. <u>More & more sure.</u>' Don had received a serious head wound while serving in the Guards during the Great War, resulting in temporary blindness. And there would have been the question of Vera's own marriage to be confronted, for Joseph Hockman would live until 1942. In the event, Vera would resolve the matter by quietly arranging to be known as Mrs Cheeseman.

Vera turned to a fresh sheet of the blue paper to make a separate list of the presents which caused such merriment and which she seems to have continued to receive as a prelude to setting up home together. There were books 'innumerable' including 'more than half the instalments for the Encyclopaedia Britannica' and gramophone records from The Tudor Shop, now somewhat in decline, in 'wholesale quantities' which were intended 'all to be transferred to Robin Hill by degrees.' Vera also listed a brooch and a straw hat, a blue enamel dressing table set, a scent spray and several clocks – Don was an expert horologist – including a 'Brass Face Lantern Clock 17th Century.' Neither was the dining room forgotten, for Vera also received such useful and choice items as grapefruit spoons, ivory afternoon tea knives and a sugar sifter of 'lovely design.'

There were two more visits over the Easter weekend, with walks in the woods and games with the children, and before long Don, a tall and distinguished-looking figure, was being introduced to relatives and friends. These included Carice, who Vera notes as saying 'I feel I have known him all my life.' The brief entries continue on an almost daily basis until nearly the end of May and record various further meetings, outings and rehearsals, including notably on Tuesday 21st 'Rehearsal 4. 30 for Uncle Ralph's Sea Symphony. We met at College. Afterwards found sweet peas in car!' A few days later the pair went away for their first weekend together, leaving from Baker Street at 5. 35 on the Friday evening. It was a sign of complete commitment: 'No regrets, only rejoicing. Next Friday as ever is!' she had written. On the day itself she noted, 'All aboard the Blue Bird for Paradise, Alton, Winchester, Petersfield, Grayshott, Hindhead, Hazelmere, Frensham Ponds, Waggoners Wells.' And she concluded by repeating the lines from Shelley's *Epipsychidion* that she had associated with the last phrases of the slow movement of the Elgar Violin Concerto. 'Henceforth,' she wrote,

"One hope within two wills, one will beneath
Two overshadowing minds, one life, one death,
One Heaven, one Hell, one immortality,
And one annihilation."

The 1935 Three Choirs Festival was at Worcester and it became necessarily imbued with a special significance. There were memorable performances of *Gerontius* and *The Apostles* and a special dedication service for an Elgar memorial window, situated in the nave near to the spot where the composer loved to stand and watch performances. Carice also arranged for the cottage at Broadheath to be open to visitors during the Festival period. Vera's signature, together with that of Don Cheeseman, is to be found in the Visitors' Book for 6th September, a few days after that of Alan Kirby. Perhaps Vera was seeking to invoke Hyperion's blessing on her new love, for life goes on.

*

As if to coincide with the Festival, Billy Reed published an article on the Third Symphony in *The Listener* of 28th August, including facsimiles of many of the sketches presented in his own ordering. This gesture has often been misunderstood, for it appears to sit very ill with Reed's own promise to Elgar that 'no one would ever tamper with it in any way, or attempt to construct what would have to be a most unsatisfactory work.' Putting the material in the public domain would surely risk exposing it to the kind of tampering that Elgar wanted so much to avoid. And if Reed's article and his subsequent republication of the sketches in his book appear at the very least not to make sense, and at the worst a betrayal of trust, it was nevertheless endorsed by Carice in a letter to Basil Maine of April 1939 in which she wrote: ' . . . it does seem to me a great safeguard for the future that the themes have been published. Perhaps I look too far ahead – but I had awful visions of people getting hold of it in about AD 2000! when there would be nobody left who would have known him, and trying to finish it.'

The reason for Reed's publication of the sketches is to be found in the financial and legal dealings over the question of the ownership of the symphony sketches between Carice and Sir John Reith of the BBC in the aftermath of Elgar's death. Reith lost little time in getting to grips with the matter. In a private memorandum of 2nd March 1934 to the head of the BBC's legal department, Jardine Brown, he succinctly outlined various options. It was evident that Landon Ronald was continuing to be an active go-between and that Carice's financial situation was a sensitive one; under the terms of her father's Will, she had been left income but no capital.

Elgar: B. B. C. payment, M.S. , etc.

Sir Edward Elgar told me in a recent letter that he had made arrangements for the return of the £1000 to us in the event of his dying before finishing the work. Of course I replied quite non-committally, and I do not feel that we could well have it back. I am told by Sir Landon Ronald that he has not left much money and that his daughter, Mrs. Blake, would be inconvenienced if she had to return the money, her husband apparently not making much of things. I do not think Mrs. Blake will take the initiative in the matter, and I understand from Sir Landon that she might be hoping to hear something from us.

If we leave the £1000 with them we are entitled to what MS. there is, and Ronald tells me there is quite an amount.

Elgar gave instructions, however, that no work was to be done on it by anyone, and Ronald suggests that we should write to Mrs. Blake asking her to send us the MS. , but giving her at the same time some legal document which ensures that nobody would try to do anything with it (except as under). I presume this will be a contract between ourselves and her, although I suppose it is open to question as to whether he was entitled to make stipulations about it and still have our £1000 retained in the family.

An alternative which Ronald suggested, but which I do not think there is much point in, was that Mrs. Blake should send us a cheque for £1000 and we should then return it in exchange for the MS., in which case she would be entitled of course to attach any legal conditions she liked to the sale; but in fact she ought not to attach any because of the amount of the cheque, which is certainly more than she would get from the British Museum, whom Ronald says are anxious to secure all his MSS. .

Ronald hopes that we shall have the MS. and put in a glass case [sic]. But if this is to be done, I said I should wish to have someone examine it and write up a decent article for publication in 'The Listener', quoting some of the themes or other significant passages from what had been done. Ronald said he saw no possible objection to this from Elgar's point of view, but that the point would have to be covered.

Please decide what is to be done and give me the necessary letters to sign – to Mrs. Blake direct if we are to communicate with her, or to Sir Landon Ronald, who in any event should be kept fully informed of what is done.

I am sure Dr. Boult would appreciate being consulted on this matter.

It was a tactful final thought. Ronald, a member of the BBC Advisory Panel, had been one of the prime movers all the way along, but Boult was the BBC's Director of Music as well as Chief Conductor of the BBC Symphony Orchestra and no less an advocate of Elgar's music. The two men seem to have been temperamentally antipathetic, however. 'Lunched with Sir Hugh Allen,' Reith had noted in his diary one day during the previous May, 'in connection with a row between Landon Ronald and Boult, Boult having been very rude to Ronald, and he having sent in his resignation.' And he had diarised too a more recent experience of conductors' infighting and the continuing ill feeling between Ronald and Boult.

25 January 1934 . . . lunched with Landon Ronald at Claridges. He told me that Hugh Allen had, on my suggestion, written a letter which the three leaders of the profession were to send to The Times in appreciation of our Music Festival, but he had included in it an appreciation of Boult. For some reason he showed this to Beecham and the latter said that if it were published with the Boult part in it he would write a letter critical of Boult. Ronald said our orch. would be infinitely better if we had a different conductor.

Reith's diary entry for 2nd March 1934 confirms his Third Symphony sketches conversation with Ronald – who certainly seems to have been a master of the business lunch – and the direction his own mind was taking over the matter.

. . . lunched with Ronald at the Langham; much conversation about Elgar. He thought that we should not say any more about Elgar's offer to have the

£1000 returned, but should write to his daughter asking for the MS of the 3rd Symphony, of which apparently there is a good deal, to be sent to us, we giving an undertaking that it would not be worked on. I told Ronald that there certainly ought to be an article written about it, probably for The Listener, giving some of the more interesting themes, etc. , which he quite agreed . . .

In other words, Reith was determined that he should have something for his money; or perhaps, more fairly, that the public should have something for theirs. And so it has proved. After a little more legal discussion, a contract was duly drawn up and signed by Carice on 20th July, 1934, in which she agreed to hand over her own rights in the Third Symphony sketches to the BBC, in return for which

> The Corporation for itself and its successors and assigns hereby undertakes and agrees that none of the said manuscripts shall ever be published either in whole or in part and that they will not permit any person whatever to have access to the said manuscripts for the purpose of finishing or completing or making any alteration PROVIDED ALWAYS that nothing herein contained shall be construed as preventing the Corporation from publishing an article in "The Listener" relative to the said manuscripts in which some of the themes or other significant passages may be quoted.

And so the arrangement was legally confirmed at Reith's insistence, and Reed's article duly appeared.

*

Carice picked up the threads of her diary again at the beginning of 1936, and kept it until the end of December 1939, after which point her life changed completely, in common with those of so many of her countrymen and women of all sorts and conditions. But her immediate preoccupations were somewhat nearer home as Sam's health continued poor and more and more time, thought and energy had to be devoted to the plans for establishing a permanent museum at her father's birthplace at Broadheath. The Worcester Corporation bought the cottage in May, 1935, and shortly afterwards a public appeal for funds to help with running costs was launched through the *Daily Telegraph* under the chairmanship of Landon Ronald. Atkins, Boult, Reed and Vaughan Williams were among the signatories. Carice made it her business to plan the layout of the rooms and collect together the correspondence, press cuttings, manuscripts, books, photographs and personal memorabilia which remain today the heart of the Elgar Archive. She also had to decide on and obtain the most appropriate furniture for the museum. Various friends helped, including Charlotte Shaw, who assisted in the putting up of some curtains on one occasion.

Her friendship with Vera did not die, since over the next two years Carice continued to use Robin Hill as a base for London visits. She spent a long weekend with Vera in the spring of 1936, taking in an Elgar performance at Southwark Cathedral, Mass at Brompton Oratory, and discussions over the Birthplace fund. The last day included an outing with Vera:

Monday 2 March 1936. Vera & I to Chinese Art Exhibition & Fortnum and Mason for tisanes. Lunch & home by 4 . . . Sam had had nosebleed but seemed all right . . .

Towards the end of April Carice met Vera for lunch in Dorking and sat next to Dulcie while Vaughan Williams rehearsed the Verdi *Requiem* in the afternoon. Afterwards Vera drove her up Westcott Road, so they could see The White Gates, the bungalow where the composer had chosen to live in order to make matters easier for his arthritic wife Adeline. And in May there was another sentimental journey: 'Vera to lunch & tea went to Brinkwells.' It was the cottage at nearby Fittleworth where Elgar had written the Violin Sonata ('My Sonata – Our Sonata') that Vera had played with the composer on her first visit to Marl Bank ssome four and a half years before. Carice no doubt told much of their somewhat rustic life there towards the end of the First World War and afterwards. Vera, with her imaginative quick sympathy, would have been entranced by the special atmosphere of the cottage and its place in Elgar's creative life. The two women met again at the Three Choirs Festival, and later in December they shared a London performance of *Gerontius*:

Wednesday 2 December 1936. Sam bad cold – rested after lunch. Went to London for Gerontius. Met Vera at Club & gave her dinner not good – but we enjoyed it. Stayed with her.

Next year Carice spent another long weekend at Robin Hill in February, including another 'lovely evening with records etc,' and a light-hearted invitation from the Reeds; 'Vera & Don & Dulcie to supper. Played quotations.' There was another joint venture to London in the summer and Vera went to the Malvern Festival in August, but Carice makes no further mention of her for the rest of 1937 and for the whole of 1938. The Elgar Birthplace Museum was permanently opened that year and Carice and Sam moved to Broadheath so that the undertaking could be properly supervised.

*

It was becoming more and more difficult to ignore the worrying developments in Europe which were becoming a more and more pervasive background to everybody's life during the thirties. Nazi persecution of Jewish intellectuals had been noted by Elgar himself in a letter of March 1933 to Adela Schuster, the 'very tall and gaunt and silver-haired' old lady who had so impressed Vera on her visit to Wimbledon. She was Jewish, just as Vera was:

> I am hoping that you have been able to enjoy the wonderful weather which has made the earth look like a promise of better things; – I fear not of better times though: I am in a maze regarding events in Germany – what are they doing? In this morning's paper it is said that the greatest conductor Bruno Walter &, stranger still, Einstein are ostracised: are we all mad? The Jews have always been my best & kindest friends – the pain of these news is unbearable & I do not know what it really means.

He sensed the worst, but did not live to see it. Vaughan Williams also sensed what was coming, and was able to issue warnings, conscious or otherwise, in his magnificent, dissonant and violent Fourth Symphony of 1935 and the cantata *Dona Nobis Pacem* of 1936. It was a characteristic response from a composer whose philosophy of life committed him, in his own words, to cultivating 'a sense of musical citizenship' and making of his art 'an expression of the whole life of the community.' He thought very carefully before accepting an award from Hamburg University in 1937, pointing out that he was strongly opposed to the German system of government, 'especially with regard to its treatment of artists and scholars,' and adding too that he belonged 'to more than one English society whose object is to combat all that the present German *régime* stands for.'

Gradually the trickle of refugees of all kinds – racial and political – became a flood as the persecution intensified, and when in the December of 1938 the Dorking Committee for Refugees from Nazi Oppression was set up, Vaughan Williams became an active member. Early in February 1939 – by which time his music had been banned in Germany – the composer wrote to Vera, not for the first time it would seem, to ask her help in raising money. He was appealing on this occasion so that a German-Jewish architect and his family could take ship for safety in New Zealand. Dr. Fuchs had come to England at the private invitation of some Dorking friends and was therefore not eligible for assistance from public funds.

The White Gates,
Westcott Road,
Dorking.

Feb 3 [1939]

My Dearest Vera,

This is frankly a begging letter – & I hate doing it because I know that your generous heart has already helped, more than you ought, these unfortunates & you must be frank with me & say "no" & I shall quite understand. You will see all about Dr. Fuchs on the other sheet.

I have already had some generous answers & have been able to add about £100 to what we already had, making altogether about £300 more wanted.

Love from Uncle Ralph

*

For Carice, the final declaration of the war that everyone had expected for so long and the sad outcome of her husband's increasing infirmity came almost together. Sam Blake died on 29th August 1939 at the same South Bank Nursing Home in Worcester where her father had been tended; it must have been hard for Carice to retrace her steps there, with inevitable memories of the sufferings of five years before. The day of the cremation itself brought bad news:

Friday 1st September 1939. Mr. & Mrs. Ellis came with me to Woking Crematorium. Told about Germany making war on Poland exactly as the coffin was brought in.

The day of Neville Chamberlain's famous broadcast saw Carice carrying on as usual, visiting some old family friends, the Leicesters.

Sunday 3rd September 1939. Outbreak of war announced at 11. Went to lunch with Nella & Philip.

Later in December Carice took train to London for a pre-Christmas meeting with Vera. They lunched at the M. M. Club, a little basement affair next to Oxford Circus tube station run by the cellist May Mukle, a favourite haunt of many distinguished musicians including 'Uncle Ralph.' And she particularly remembered that New Year's Eve, when she had gone to stay at Windsor with another old friend, Clare Stuart Wortley.

Sunday 31 December 1939 . . . To Mass at 11. Reading letters. To Service at 3 – sat in organ loft. Last item played in St. George's Windsor in 1939 was the Nimrod . . .

*

With the passing of another year it became evident that the 'phoney war' was over. France and the Low Countries fell to Hitler, followed by the evacuation from Dunkirk, the Battle of Britain and the first bombing raids on London. Don and Vera made their contribution to ARP work, but on one occasion while on duty in a trench, part of it collapsed and some sandbags fell on Vera's head. It was always thought by her family that this incident was at the root of the cruel illness which affected her later.

Wartime experiences concentrated minds in all kinds of ways. Vera dated her manuscript of *Elgar and Poetry* 'Christmas 1940,' and she seems to have been thinking a good deal about her Hyperion at this time, being drawn again to the Worcester area. On New Year's Day she revisited the cottage at Broadheath and she signed the Visitors' Book once more. In a tiny gesture that would have meant so much to her while being probably entirely overlooked by others, she gave her address as 'Robin Hill, Pine Coombe, Shirley, *Corydon.*' And in the early years of the War, with her own children growing up and leaving the nest, Vera adopted another child, a daughter, Nina. The new baby brought happiness and fulfilment for one to whom the rôle of mother came so naturally and provided a focus of hope for the future in the grim uncertain days of conflict.

During the 1914-18 War, Carice's gift for languages had enabled her to work in the Censorship. Now she remained at Broadheath, on hand to help the curators of the Birthplace, which came in wartime to take on something of the special symbolism of a national shrine. She helped, too, to run a canteen for servicemen and women at St. George's Catholic Church in Worcester, where her father and grandfather had been organists. Here in 1941 she first met Sybil Russell, a member of the Women's Royal Air Force billeted at Marl Bank. Sybil was a good enough cellist to play with local orchestras. Although at thirty-nine she was some twelve years younger than Carice, who was fifty-one that year, the two women became intimate friends, with music and dogs as shared interests. After Sybil had been invalided out of the Services, the pair set up home together at Broadheath. It would prove a lifelong partnership and one that brought Carice perfect happiness. Sybil's practical energies were immediately put towards the Birthplace cause. She remembered:

> When I first joined Carice, after leaving the Air Force, we were both in total agreement that the Birthplace should become better known by the music public. This suggested to me that as the Birthplace was in such a remote spot, it should be publicised as having a convenient place to rest – possibly a tea-room. Carice owned land opposite, so we searched for a portable

building. Luckily we found one, and quite soon it was erected. Fittings were difficult to come by, and decorative curtains quite impossible. Luckily I was able to secure some plain material suitable for my fabric painting, and lastly, we secured a dozen small tables and suitable chairs. Not long after we opened the public began to show considerable interest to visit the small cottage, which was, of course, of great interest to Elgar lovers . . . As the public became aware of the amenity we more than doubled the number of visitors. Later I secured a reasonably large board, and painted 'Birthplace Tea-Room' which also served light meals when required.

*

'Business as usual' was the cry in music-making as in so much else at this time. Although the Croydon Philharmonic Society's strength was severely depleted by the call-up and evacuation, a small core of local people attended 'drop in and sing' sessions on Saturday afternoons and six concerts, including a deeply moving *Messiah,* were given in the first three years of the war. Characteristically, Alan Kirby built on his success and moulded his forces as best he could, attracting singers from other defunct choirs and making use of Service men and women on leave. Indefatigably he mounted *The Kingdom* in 1943 and *The Apostles* in 1944. It was the only performance that either work received in those years. In 1943, too, the Croydon Philharmonic joined forces with the LSO in a memorial concert for Billy Reed, who had died suddenly the previous year. There is no doubt that Vera would have been saddened by the loss of an unforgettable friend and personality with so many Elgarian memories and associations for her.

Vaughan Williams, too old now to join up and serve as he had in the Great War, continued to make a full and energetic contribution to the war effort in Dorking, helping to organise allotments, air-raid shelters and salvage collections, and practising fire-fighting as well as continuing his letter-writing and committee work on behalf of refugees. He was appointed Chairman of the Home Office Committee for the Release of Interned Alien Musicians, and also attended meetings of the Department of National Service Entertainment whose headquarters were at the Theatre Royal, Drury Lane. For one such meeting, on 7th May, 1942, he was sent an official railway voucher for the journey from Dorking. Wartime conditions were all-pervasive; 'IMPORTANT,' ran the rubric of instruction for typists at the bottom of the page, 'In the National interest please use both sides, single spacing and full width of paper.' Only too anxious to obey the spirit of the law, V.W. used the back of the page for a frank note to Vera, who had evidently asked his help in seeking publication for her writings about Elgar. With characteristic and refreshing bluntness, Vaughan Williams used the occasion to demolish two Elgarian sacred cows. Vera had sent compliments about *Hugh the Drover*, which the composer referred to as a 'tune,' a term he delighted in using about his major works.

Dearest Vera,

I am sending your script to the Musical Times. That horrible woman "Dorabella" has queered the pitch for reminiscences – also that dreadful book by Basil Maine!

My dear how sweet of you to write about Hugh. I am so glad when you like my tunes.

All my love

Uncle Ralph

But unconventional reminiscences such as Vera's were evidently of no interest to the learned journal, even with the endorsement of the leading figure in English music, for they were not published. Two years later she seems to have tried *Music & Letters,* at that time under the editorship of the writer and critic Eric Blom, but the result was the same. Still loth to give up, Vera again sought the endorsement of an important figure, this time the distinguished singer and administrator, Steuart Wilson. He replied,

I like this paper very much, but I can see Eric Blom's dilemma as a publisher. It *is* so personal to you, though it is "generally" true. The many-faceted-man shows himself to everyone different, but we also see ourselves reflected in him.

Whether such a response amounted to a genuine psychological insight or a patronising put-down, it would seem that the times were not right for the publication of Vera's Elgarian writings. 'I knew him,' she had written, and there could be no inhibition or embarrassment for Vera in that knowing, whatever the reactions of others. And it is difficult to imagine that she had not shown her reminiscences to Carice and gained approval for her efforts to share them with a wider readership.

In the middle of the war, Vaughan Williams produced another symphony, his fifth, given its first performance in June 1943. Its serene beauty came like a benediction in grim times, and Vera wrote to praise it, as did many friends. In reply there was a self-deprecating anecdote:

The White Gates,
Dorking.

July 7 [1943]

My Dearest Verissima,

It was most sweet of you to write. I thought everyone wd. find my new tune so dull!

Talking of large families I will tell you an amusing story. I have a young friend with no money & a growing family. He wrote that he had lately been feeling depressed & wondering whether he ought to have brought all his offspring into the world – but then my symphony had put "new hope" into him. Shall I be responsible if it mounts up to a dozen? And shall I have to support them?

All my love & to Dulcie also

Uncle Ralph

*

In February 1948 Bernard Shaw, then aged ninety-two, wrote to Lord Reith to offer what he called 'a peep behind the scenes' over the Third Symphony for the retired Director-General's autobiography. It is an extraordinary letter by any standards and one which seems never to have been quoted in any discussion of Shaw and Elgar. It began with flattery. Reith had been consistently passed over for the kind of job he felt he was capable of during the war: Churchill famously referred to him as a 'Wuthering Height.'

> You cannot deplore your departure from the B. B. C. more than I did; for I knew by long political observation that though in this country one gets to the front as an able man of action, once there his only way to political power is to convince the Government that he will not use it to do anything that can possibly be left undone. Macdonald began as the most intransigent Socialist in the movement. He became P. M. as what Beatrice Webb called him: a facade. Baldwin could be trusted to promise everything and do nothing but get photographed with a pipe in his mouth.
>
> You have never shaken off your reputation as a man of action; and nothing but another war will ever make you a P. M. It took that to do the trick for Lloyd George and Churchill when the foe was at the gate.

Shaw now turned to Elgar and the symphony. He deliberately belittled the music – or demonstrated his lack of judgement over it – and demonstrated too a complete lack of understanding of the nature of Elgar's medical condition. In seeking to exonerate Reith from any responsibility over the whole symphony venture, was Shaw, with half an eye on the forthcoming memoirs and his own posthumous reputation, trying to put himself above reproach?

> The Elgar affair was magnificent on your part; but on his it was a failure. He tried to compose a symphony, and produced a few scraps which he played for me at his house in Worcester, where I was a frequent visitor: he playing the piano and Reid [sic] (Billy Reid now dead) the fiddle. I could make neither head nor tail of the stuff. There was certainly no big theme in it.

> The fact is he was dying. For some years, his spine had been visibly going wrong, getting humped at the neck. My wife urged him to consult an osteopath; but no persuasion could induce him to resort to a doctor who was not on the British register: that was his sort of snobbery. It cost him his life.

Next came the question of the money that he had lent Elgar in 1931. Shaw broached the matter to Reith in somewhat brutal terms which mixed backstabbing with slur and innuendo.

> He was given to complaining that his fame made people expect him to work *honoris causa* and left him unpaid and in want of money. I told him that my business as a playwright obliged me to keep a large balance at my bank for emergencies and that if he was ever at a loss up to a thousand it would make no difference to me, only to the bank. He presently wrote to me for it, alleging a domestic financial crisis. I paid up; and immediately he bought a car for £800 and made a present of it to Miss Clifford, his very attractive secretary.
> I of course wrote it off as irrecoverable; but when he died he left his daughter a settled income, but no ready money. I had to rake out my cheque and put in a claim against his estate for the thousand as a loan. It was allowed; and I transferred it to his daughter's private account and saved the situation for her.
> What he did with your donation I do not know. Probably bought a Rolls Royce with it.

Shaw behaved with undoubted generosity to Carice, but a few months after the Reith letter he repeated and exaggerated one of his charges against Elgar in a letter to the composer Rutland Boughton, who had been complaining about a pension he had been awarded:

The pension was a miracle of public recognition and leaves you nothing to complain of. Though Elgar was Master of the King's Musick I had to give him £1,000 to get him out of money troubles. Of course it was nominally a loan; but I never got it back.

When this letter was published in 1962, in Michael Hurd's book on Boughton, it understandably proved too much for Carice, who published a letter in the *Sunday Times* giving a full account of the matter, and putting the kindest construction on Shaw's complaints:

> . . . this, as it stands, gives a false impression of the manner in which my father – who had a strict conscience in such matters – handled his business affairs, I should be grateful for the opportunity to state the facts.
> In 1931, Shaw advanced Elgar £1, 000. He specifically asked that no receipt should be given because he said, in the event of his death he would not wish his executors to press for payment. As it was, Elgar died first, whereupon Shaw himself claimed repayment from my father's executors, who promptly offered the required sum. Shaw returned a receipt for the money, but with characteristic generosity asked that it should be credited to me " as a birthday present."
> It would seem, then, that when writing to Rutland Boughton Shaw had forgotten both his having asked for repayment and his generosity with the repaid sum. As my father's bankers – to whose records I have referred for confirmation of the details – state: " To say that he had not been repaid was simply untrue."

If certain of Elgar's friends questioned at the time the nature, rather than the sincerity, of his friendship for Shaw, his posthumous treachery to Elgar seems to have passed unnoticed. 'It was not a real friendship . . .' For all its apparently thriving success on the surface, theirs was a fundamentally unstable relationship between incompatibles, between one who was quintessentially a Romantic and another who was not, who was, indeed, an anti-Romantic. And for all the practical encouragement he undoubtedly gave Elgar, one wonders if such a man as Shaw was capable of providing the perfect warmth and sympathy that the composer needed to inspire him. Though his illness ultimately negated her 'human spark,' there is no doubt that it was Vera's love that had sustained Elgar in his final creative efforts.

*

Vera died in March, 1963, after many years of suffering from Parkinson's Disease. The illness had started to manifest itself soon after the War. With little possibility of remediation through drugs at that time, her illness followed its classic pattern, with a stiffening of the muscles which gradually reduced the face to a mask and the voice to a monotone, rigidity of the limbs and a tremor of the hands and arms. For one who had been capable of achieving a unique quality of rapport and empathy with others, the resulting isolation and difficulties of communication would have proved hard to bear. Increasingly frail, she could move and speak only slowly, and violin playing and music making would have been an early casualty. But sheer strength of character meant that she was reluctant to talk about her own problems, and her sympathetic interest in others remained as strong as it had always been. For those who knew and loved Vera, her special presence and beauty shone through the distorted features and remain vivid and precious in the memory to this day. Sylvia Disley, Don Cheeseman's daughter by his earlier marriage, remembered:

> I very much admired Vera for the stoic, and heroic, way she coped with her illness. It was typical of her that she once described her illness to me as "unimportant." Eventually there was very little she could do for herself and when she made her last visit to my home (after I was married) she told me not to worry when I had to help her to the bathroom, as, she told me, "I have no pride left." She dealt with her final illness with fortitude, dignity and courage. I remember her sitting in an armchair, hardly able to hold herself up, and yet pointing out the beauty of a tree which she could see through the window. It was so typical of Vera only to see the beauty and goodness of everything and everyone around her no matter how bad she felt.

Vera and Don had remained a closely devoted couple. On one occasion she was so pleased to see him after a few days away on a visit to Dulcie that she wept when he came to collect her. The long drawn-out illness inevitably proved a strain for Don, and led to the sacrifice of his orchestral playing:

> I recall him telling me . . . that playing with the orchestra was the one thing that helped him forget, just for a while, the very real worry that he was going through at home. In the end, when she became so ill that he had to give up his playing in order to be with her all the time, even though they had a housekeeper, he did not tell her that he had voluntarily given up his position in the orchestra, and said that he had simply been replaced. This was not true, but he did not want Vera to feel bad about him having to give up his position in the orchestra for her sake. But with competition for places in an orchestra such as the Royal Philharmonic, my father must have known that once he left the orchestra it would be difficult to get back in again even though he had been a founder member of the R. P. O. and Sir Thomas Beecham had asked him to form the double bass section for him when it

was first formed in the late forties . . . During her final illness my father lost a lot of weight and looked as if he was heading for a nervous breakdown, and after she died he was naturally inconsolable.

Vera's expressed wish was that she should be was cremated 'in as simple a fashion as possible.' She had accumulated a suitcase case full of letters from Elgar, and left it to Don to decide their fate. He thought it best to burn them.

He told me that he was aware of the small suitcase which was full of letters from Elgar, and which she kept in the back of a wardrobe. He told me she had told him to do what he thought best with them, after her death, and that she didn't mind what he did with them. Whether that is true or not I don't know, but he described how he took the case, (he held his hands out to demonstrate its size and I could see that the case was quite big, larger than an attaché case, about two foot by eighteen inches by six inches, so there must have been a lot of letters in it) and he put the whole lot, case and all, on the bonfire.

Elgar seems to have taken equal care that none of his letters from Vera have come down to us. We will naturally regret the loss, but Vera had preserved what she wanted to preserve of her precious intimacy with the composer in her 'Story.' The rest truly might have been silence, had not Tony Payne brought Vera and Elgar's love of her back to life through the serene beauty of her own theme in the Third Symphony. To paraphrase Elgar's own words, the music is a part of them both – and now we share.

Vera with her granddaughter Marion and adopted daughter Nina, together with
Dulcie's husband's mother, c.1945

Vera, Dulcie and Marion in the garden at Robin Hill

TELEPHONE
DORKING 355.

THE WHITE GATES,
WESTCOTT ROAD,
DORKING.

p.s. Do you think Mr Blake would write me a line to pass on to Ursula dear?

Dear Ursula

How wonderful to see you & write once more.

I love having all your dear letters round me making music with her devotion to the art — it is a great experience for me.

I wanted to embrace you all — but the occasion was too public

Mr Blake was so wonderfully sympathetic we must carry our own plan on Wednesday early in June

Love from Uncle Ralph

A letter from 'Uncle Ralph'

DEPARTMENT OF NATIONAL SERVICE ENTERTAINMENT

CORRESPONDENCE IN REPLY TO THIS
LETTER SHOULD BE ADDRESSED
TO THE

**DIRECTOR OF NATIONAL
SERVICE ENTERTAINMENT
(....ENSA. A. M. C..)**

AND REF........................QUOTED

HEADQUARTERS:

**THEATRE ROYAL,
DRURY LANE, LONDON,
W.C.2.**

TELEPHONE:
TEMPLE BAR 1575.

TELEGRAMS:
" DRURIOLANUS, RAND,
LONDON."

DATE..APRIL....30th.
1942.

Dr. R. Vaughan-Williams,
Whitegates,
Westcot Road,
DORKING, Surrey.

Dear Dr. Vaughan-Williams:

Re. Meeting of the A.M.C. on
Thursday May 7th at 11. 15 a.m.

    I have pleasure in enclosing herewith your
railway voucher for the above named meeting. If
you will present this at the booking office you
will receive a railway ticket in return. Although
the voucher is dated the 7th May, you can of course
travel on the day before that date.

    With kind regards,

               Yours sincerely,

               Scy. WALTER LEGGE
               L.O. A. M. C.

Enc.

IMPORTANT.—In the National interest please use both sides, single spacing and full width of paper.

Railway pass for a composer

V.W. at the Hereford Festival, 1933

V.W. and Percy Hull at the Worcester Festival, 1932

Don Cheeseman at rehearsal

SIR EDWARD ELGAR BURIED.—The coffin of Sir Edward Elgar, the famous composer, being carried from the church to the grave at yesterday's simple funeral at Little Malvern. He was buried by the side of Lady Elgar, who died fourteen years ago.

'They all got to know.' Elgar's funeral, a newspaper photograph

Appendix

'You'll never leave me, will you? '

Another most touching example of Elgar and the Eternal Feminine is to be found in his relationship with Kathleen Harrison, a part-time nurse at the South Bank Nursing Home where Elgar stayed from October 1933 to January 1934. Such was her relationship with the dying composer and his daughter that Nurse Harrison was asked to continue to care for him when he was moved back to Marl Bank; she herself lived close by on Rainbow Hill and was able to nurse Elgar through January and February 1934 – including the day of the celebrated land-line recordings of excerpts from Caractacus *– and up until the day of his death. Many years later, as a very old lady in a nursing home herself, Kathleen Harrison recorded some reminiscences of this period for a local radio programme, 'Memories of Elgar,' which I have transcribed for this appendix. Although certain of her recollections – the time of Elgar's death, for example – are at variance with the information given in other documented sources, some others are poignant, revealing and uniquely suggestive. She began by talking about an invitation from the Matron to help out at South Bank and her first meeting with Carice and her father, the day before the exploratory operation which revealed the extent of his cancer. They were evidently anxious that he should be consistently nursed by the same person as much as possible, not by a succession of different staff on shifts.*

One day I had a message from her to say can you come and help us out, so I said well, I thought – oh dear I was going away for the weekend – so I said yes, I can come. Well, so I said when I got there, what do you want me to do? She said help wherever they're busy, and I went into one room, and I was helping this gentleman, and a lady said –

"My father's having his operation tomorrow and we want you to be his 'special.' "

- nursing him all the time you see, and I said I can't, I don't belong here, I'm just called in to help. So I thought, oh well, in any case the other staff wouldn't like it. But anyway the next morning I was detailed off to look after Sir Edward. That was the first time that I met him, a sick person in bed in a ward in South Bank Nursing Home. I didn't realise who he was, although he lived so near to me, on Rainbow Hill, not very far from where I was. You see I didn't really know him. My friends that lived in a house opposite they used to talk to him a lot – he and his doggy. I heard a friend say, well didn't you know him before, and I said no, and they said well if you'd gone into town sometimes you'd have seen Sir Edward and his secretary coming out with an ice cream. He loved to go for an ice cream, I didn't know that.

He was a poorly man, and I gave him a drink, and took his temperature. And then I saw him next morning from the theatre, and he had his operation and I nursed him at South Bank Nursing Home for three months, and then we took him home to Marl Bank, Rainbow Hill, where I nursed him until he died.

Nurse Harrison's commitment to her patient led to a degree of exhaustion which she was unable to conceal from Elgar's doctor, Moore Ede, son of the Dean of Worcester. It led to a pathetic exchange between patient and nurse.

I used to talk to him quite a lot you know and I remember one day, oh dear, he was so poorly. He had trouble with his back, you see, and I was rubbing his back, and oh, I am so tired, and I walked over to the dressing table, and he said,

"My dear, I may be a troublesome old man, but I am in a lot of pain, you know."

And I said, "I know you are. I've only come over here for a change!"

But he was a sick man . . . and Dr. Moore Ede said,

"How is he now?"

And I said, "He's not very well this morning."

We went in to see Sir Edward, and then we came out and we had gone out on the landing, and he said,

"You're not very well."

And I said, "I'm all right!"

He said, "You're not all right – no good telling me you're all right, 'cos you're not!"

So I said, "Well, I had a very bad night."

So we went back in to Sir Edward, and he said,

"Sir Edward, you're killing your poor dear sister, you're wearing her out."

I went back in the bedroom, and he said, "Come here, my dear."

And he held my hand, and he said, "You'll never leave me, will you?"

And I said, "Never."

He said, "You are sure you will never leave me?"

And I said, "Never."

Kathleen Harrison went on to give an account in her own inimitable style of the recordings that Elgar supervised from his bed at Marl Bank on 22nd January, 1934. Elgar was receiving frequent injections of morphia and the resulting drowsiness meant that his ability to carry the project through was in some doubt until almost the last moment.

And they fitted it all up, all the contraptions, to help Sir Edward to hear some of his music, to see if it could be broadcast, you see. He was so ill that day, and Dr. Moore Ede said to me,

"How is he?"

And I said, "I don't know, I don't know how he's going through with it."

And he said, "Oh well, we'll wait and see."

And presently he came to knock at the door to tell me he was ready, and he was fast asleep. I said,

"Sir Edward –"

"Yes, my dear, what is it?"

And I said, "They're waiting for you in London."

"Oh give me my doings."

And he sat up in bed, and he got his baton, and he sat up with all the music, and he listened to all the music. All the contraptions were there, you know. And Billy Reed said,

"Is that all right?"

"No," he said. "I want so-and-so and so-and-so altered."

And he said, "Alright we'll try again."

So they played the music again, and he said,

"Is that all right?"

"No," he said, "I want so-and-so and so-and-so, and he got his baton and he did all this business, and then they did play it again, and they said,

"Is that better?"

"That's all right."

For much of the time during his last weeks and days Elgar was in a very muddled mental condition. '. . . he is in a state of quite frightful mental confusion – which is a most dreadful state of things to deal with,' wrote Carice, and on another occasion she described her father as living in a world of the most 'extraordinary dreams.' It was perhaps only fitting for a composer who had made dreams into something of a byword in his work. It was evident that his mind continued full of music, and that the sounds he heard in his imagination were so vivid as to blur the distinctions between dream and reality.

He said one day to me, "What are they playing?"

And I said, "They're not playing anything."

"Oh they are, my dear."

I said, "They're not. There isn't a piano or anything, there's nothing on the radio. No, they're not playing anything."

"Are you sure," he said. "Oh, my dear child, it's in this silly old head of mine. Of course you can't hear it."

He often said that. A lot of the time he was a bit sort of dopey, you know.

And he talked about a little girl, an unidentifiable 'dream child.' Could it perhaps have been Dulcie, or indeed the illegitimate daughter that William Walton

and Lord Clark believed existed? Then Nurse Harrison added a vignette of Carice under all the pressure.

He said something about a little girl, but he didn't have a little girl, he only had Mrs Blake, the daughter.

Carice came to South Bank regularly. She lived on Rainbow Hill – Marl Bank, you see – and when I'd finished work at South Bank I used to call on her at night, and go and have a chat with her and tell her what had happened during the day, you see.

So there we were, she was propped up in bed and we were both drinking sherry and chatting about what had happened during the day. You see, really, very often in those days it isn't the patient, it was very often the relatives that worry you, you see. They want to know everything that happened – bit tiring.

Kathleen Harrison's memories finish with her account of Elgar's death, before which he received a visit from a priest who 'ministered to him such sacraments as he could receive.' Her close interest in the patient led her to develop more and more a kind of sixth sense about his condition.

I never really knew that he was a Roman Catholic, although I nursed him for three months in South Bank. I never realised that he was a Roman Catholic, never.

It happened very often in the night, I know. I used to have a bad night, and my mother would say,

"Oh, you have been restless and talking. You had a bad night."

I said, "I know I have."

She said, "I guarantee there's somebody – that Sir Edward's been ill in the night."

And sure enough, when I got there that had happened in the night, you see, it was all upsetting me, you see. But I don't ever remember the priest coming to the house while I was there, never.

I was on day duty, I wasn't on night duty, and I said to Mrs Blake, she said,

"How is he today?"

And I said, "Not very well at all."

She said, "Oh dear."

And I said, "Well now, don't worry, nurse won't mind. I'll stay with her, we'll both be on tonight."

And so we stayed together all night, and the next morning he was better. So she said,

"How is he?"

And I said, "Well, he's revived, seems better."

So I was at work all day and then at night she said,

"What about tonight?"

I said, "Well, I'm not going to stay tonight, I think he'll be all right."

So the next night she said, "What about it?"

And I said, "Oh, I'll stay tonight," and I take two more nights and the third night he died, you see. He died in the middle of the night. We were both there. Then he was on drugs of course all the time to cure the pain because he was in such agonising pain. I were there with him. He just died. He didn't say anything, or anything like that; he was unconscious really with the drugs. I think they do get a lot like that, you know, dopey.

I called her in. Oh yes, and I sent for the doctor as well – sent for all of them. I can remember now, what was his name, saying,

"And the pen that used to write that will write no more."

We did what we always did, the both of us, but we first got the doctor to see him. And I know in the morning I went home, my mother said,

"What's the matter? Anybody would think it was your nearest and dearest, you're so upset."

I mean I used to go every day, and arrange the flowers in his room after he died. I was with him all the time.

Elgar's funeral took place on the morning of Monday 26th February at St. Wulstan's Church, Little Malvern. It was intended to be a purely private internment, with no mourning worn, and for flowers just a single bunch of daffodils. That Kathleen Harrison was invited to join the small group of relatives and friends who attended is some recognition perhaps of the devotion with which she had nursed her patient. She reminds us that the ceremony became somewhat more public than was intended. Photographs subsequently appeared in the newspapers.

Nobody was supposed to know about it, we were all supposed to be quiet. So it was arranged that I should walk, I should go down the town and meet Dr. Moore Ede on the cross by the International. That's where I met him, and we went over to Malvern. All the other different people went from different parts so nobody should know what was going on, but when we got into the road just by the Church, it was absolutely crowded with people. They all got to know.

Notes

Abbreviations used

BBC   BBC Written Archives Centre, Caversham Park, Reading.

BS   Bernard Shaw Collected Letters 1926-1950, ed. Laurence. Viking 1988.

CL.   Edward Elgar, A Creative Life. J. N. Moore, OUP 1984.

EAF   The Elgar-Atkins Friendship. E. W. Atkins, David & Charles 1984.

EE.   Edward Elgar, His Life and Music. Diana M. McVeagh, Dent 1955.

ELW   Edward Elgar, His Life and Works. Basil Maine, New Portway Edition 1972

EoR   Elgar on Record. J. N. Moore, OUP 1974.

LoL   Edward Elgar, Letters of a Lifetime, ed. J. N. Moore. Clarendon Press Oxford 1990

LoW   Letters of Edward Elgar, and Other Writings, ed. P. M. Young. Geoffrey Bles 1956.

WVW The Works of Ralph Vaughan Williams 2nd Edition. Michael Kennedy, OUP 1980.

Pages xv-xvi

As you came from the holy land is quoted in the modernised version given in *The New Oxford Book of Sixteenth Century Verse*, ed. Jones. OUP 1991. See also *The White Goddess,* Robert Graves, Fourth Edition, ed. Lindop, Faber 1999, pp. 482 and 502 – 3.

Introduction: The Courage to Defy Convention

Page 1

"All I have done was owing to her . . ." CL p. 755

". . . the old artistic 'striving' world exists for me no more . . ." LoW p. 266

"I have tried to take up the old life . . ." EE p. 70

". . . Elgar turned to him and said . . ." Ian Parrott, *The Spiritual Pilgrims*, Walters, Pembrokeshire, 1964, p. 62.

Page 2

". . . my wife loved your things." LoL p. 370

". . . when the composer and he were guests . . ." ELW pp. 44- 45.

Page 3

". . . he talked of the recent burglary . . ." LoL pp 447-448.

Page 4

"After some pondering he replied . . ." Anecdotes communicated by Nina Driver.

"Like all highly-strung human beings . . ." *Readings of Elgar*, Ernest Newman, *Sunday Times,* 6 November, 1955.

"Sir, – In the "Times Literary Supplement of February 18th" *Worcester Daily Times,* 15th March 1926.

Page 5

"Sir, – A letter in your issue of March 15 is so strange" *Ibid.* , 16th March, 1926.

Page 6

"Sir, – Sir Edward Elgar misses the point." *Ibid.* , 17th March, 1926.

"It will be a great thing . . ." Quoted in EAF, p. 408

"I don't see (really) what else he *could* say . . ." *Ibid.* , p. 409

Page 7

"How wonderful is Death." The Shelley extracts have been taken from the Oxford Standard Author Series, ed. Hutchinson, OUP. 2nd. Edition, 1970.

Page 9

"I would rather not have my name connected . . ." LoL p. 448.

". . . I again met Shaw at the Olivier's house . . ." G. F. McClearly, *Some Early Recollections of GBS, Fortnightly Review*, February 1953. Quoted in *Shaw: Interviews and Recollections,* ed. Gibbs, Macmillan 1990. *The Admirable Bashville* was written and published in 1901 and first performed in 1902.

". . . expected nothing from any English composer . . ." G. B. Shaw, *Sir Edward Elgar. Music & Letters*, January 1920.

Page 10

"Bernard Shaw is hopelessly wrong . . ." Letter from Elgar to Troyte Griffith, 14/7/1904. LoW, p. 138.

". . . a poor play . . ." *Ibid.* , p. 177

". . . the intolerable tedium of sitting unoccupied . . ." Corno di Bassetto, *Gas and Gaiters, The Star*, 16 May 1890. Quoted in *Shaw's Music* ed. Laurence, Second Revised Edition. Vol. II pp. 67 – 68. Bodley Head, 1981

Page 11

". . . I apologise to posterity . . ." *Daily News* 9th June 1922. *Ibid.* , Vol III pp. 729-730.

". . . during the Malvern Festival of 1929 . . ." *Worcester Daily Times*, 19th August, 1929.

"GBS's politics are, to me, appalling . . ." LoL, p. 359.

"Your turn now." Shaw to Elgar, 2/1/1929. *Ibid.* , p. 417.

Page 12

"I asked Shaw whether Elgar had been a very devout Roman Catholic." Hesketh Pearson, *Bernard Shaw, His Life and Personality,* Methuen 1961 ed. , p. 384

". . . after Lady Elgar's death . . ." *Shaw and Elgar,* by Ronald Taylor, in *Elgar Studies*, ed. Monk, Scolar Press 1990, pp. 219 – 220.

"I remember GBS and Elgar once discussing inspiration . . ." *The Times*, 31st August 1959. Elgar Birthplace Cuttings Book.

"The two men could behave like a pair of schoolboys . . ." Anecdotes contributed by Nina Driver.

Page 13

"The 'Severn Suite' is all balls, of course." Letter from Philip Heseltine to E. J. Moeran, 6/10/1930. *From Parry to Britten, English Music in Letters 1900-1945,* ed. Foreman, Batsford 1987, pp. 139-140

"It was not the first Elgar concert of the season . . ." Elgar Birthplace Cuttings Book.

Page 14

"I go to College for lesson with Ireland, but he doesn't turn up . . ." Diary of Benjamin Britten, 2/10/1930. Britten – Pears Library, Aldeburgh. This quotation from the diary of Benjamin Britten is c copyright the Trustees of the Britten-Pears Foundation and may not be further reproduced without the written permission of the Trustees.

". . . at least partially based on earlier material . . ." The whereabouts of the sketches of the *Nursery Suite* are unknown. Christopher Kent, *Edward Elgar, A Guide to Research.* Garland Publishing 1993, p. 351.

"The composer may call this nursery music . . ." Elgar Birthplace Cuttings Book.

". . . visibly flushing with pleasure . . ." Alan Webb, *Some Personal Memories. Elgar Society Newsletter,* May 1974, pp. 21 – 24.

Page 15

"Tell Delius I grow more like Falstaff . . ." Eric Fenby, *Delius as I Knew Him.* Faber and Faber 1981, p. 113.

Page 16

"Kirby and his Philharmonic . . ." Quoted in *Croydon Times,* 17/10/1958.

"May I be allowed to supplement . . ." *The Times,* 25/5/1959.

"To hear him direct . . ." *The Musical Times,* July 1959, p. 398

Page 17

"*Information and Instructions to Members of the Chorus,*" Alan Kirby and W. C. Berwick Sayers for the Third Croydon Triennial Festival 1931. Elgar Birthplace Museum. Berwick Sayers was the Croydon Borough Librarian and biographer of Samuel Coleridge-Taylor.

"Music Festival. Some Notes on Next Week's Event" *Croydon Advertiser,* 9/11/1931. Croydon Festival Archive, Local Studies Dept., Croydon Library.

Page 18

"Sir Edward Elgar. Great Reception on arrival at Croydon." *Croydon Times,* 9/11/ 1931. Croydon Festival Archive.

Page 19

"The entire company stood up . . ." *Croydon Advertiser,* 14/11/1931. Croydon Festival Archive.

Chapter 1 The Story of November 7th, 1931.

Page 20 *et seq.*

The background information about Vera and her husband that I have most gratefully used here and throughout has been supplied by her adopted daughter Nina and by other relatives and descendants. I have further footnoted other such material only when it seemed necessary.

Page 21

". . . while having a house, Robin Hill, built at Pine Coombe nearby." Vera's love of birds and birdsong may have influenced her choice of name for the house, but it is worth noting too the house of the same name which offers Irene sanctuary from Soames in *The Forstye Saga*.

". . . *Three Mystical Songs* . . ." Presumably extracted from the *Five Mystical Songs* of 1911, and performed in the arrangement for piano and string quartet for the first time. See WVW p. 410.

Page 22

". . . she narrated her childrens' early days in home-made journals . . ." In family possession.

Page 24

". . . his daughter was known to have viewed such a possibility with dismay." Conversation of 2/6/1998 with Raymond Monk, who recalls being told this by Sybil Russell.

Page 26

"The Story of November 7th, 1931." I have edited this document from the original MS in terms of punctuation and paragraphing, while retaining Vera's occasional unorthodox capitalisations, variant spellings, and single underlinings. Capitals have been used for double underlinings and bold capitals for treble underlinings.

Page 28

"Commenting on the appropriateness of such a service . . ." *Croydon Times,* 11/11/1931.

Page 35

". . . Pragmatic Sanction." 'A decree or ordinance issued by a head of State that refers to the affairs of that State; an imperial or royal ordinance with the force of law.' (New Shorter Oxford English Dictionary).

"I took my *Pageant of English Poetry* . . ." *The Pageant of English Poetry, Being 1150 Poems and Extracts by 300 Authors*. Edited by Henry Frowde, OUP 1912.

Page 39

". . . his wife's attitude to their daughter Carice . . ." Background information about Carice has been taken from CL and *Alice Elgar, Enigma of a Victorian Lady,* by Percy Young, Dobson 1978.

Page 40

". . . there were times when it was not inconvenient . . ." Conversation with Sylvia Disley, daughter of Don Cheeseman, Vera's later partner, 27/3/2000. She remembered her father saying that Elgar 'passed Vera off' as Carice's friend.

Page 42

". . . Elgar and Vera would arrange to exchange letters through Carice." Family information.

Page 44

". . . he was not the kind of man who was naturally fond of children . . ." John remembered, 'I was in fact introduced to Elgar just once, at the Shirley Park Hotel, but I have to admit I was not cute like Dulcie . . . you will not be surprised to learn that I got the impression that to be any less interested, he would have had to fall into a coma. I did meet Carice several times and the impression was very different. V.W. also was quite affable.' Letter to the writer, 9/6/200.

Page 47

"In the packet are all the existing sketches of your Sonata." Vera's Elgar MSS were donated to the Worcester Cathedral Library by Don Cheeseman. It seems likely that the sketches were subsequently passed to the Elgar Birthplace Museum at Broadheath.

Chapter 2 V. H.'s Own Theme.

Page 64

". . . naturally, you are in my thoughts . . ." Letter from Edward Elgar to Ernest Newman, 29/12/ 1931. LoL, pp. 444 – 445.

"You know, times are not really bad." Letter from Bernard Shaw to Elgar, 7/1/1932. LoW, pp. 333 – 334.

Page 65

". . . some manuscript sketches of the Symphony . . ." *Ernest Newman, A Memoir,* Vera Newman, Putnam 1963, p. 105.

"The only thing that was clear . . ." EAF, p. 446.

"The occasion was recorded in Carice's diary . . ." Photocopies held at the Elgar Birthplace Museum.

Page 66

"I shall require strings and strings . . ." Typescript supplied by Nina Driver.

Page 67

"Why not a Financial Symphony?" Letter from Bernard Shaw to Elgar, 29/6/1932. EoR, p. 171.

". . . there is nothing to say . . ." Letter from Edward Elgar to Walter Legge, 5/8/1932. EoR, pp. 180 – 181.

Page 70

". . . Elgar and Poetry . . ." Typescript supplied by Nina Driver.

Page 75

". . . the doubts about Menuhin's suitability . . ." Family information.

Page 76

". . . bring the Third Symphony into existence . . ." Letter from Bernard Shaw to Sir John Reith, 30/ 9/1932. BS, pp. 309 – 310.

Page 77

". . . during such time as the composer . . ." Agreement between Elgar and the BBC dated 9th December, 1932. BBC.

". . . whatever happens . . ." Letter from Elgar to Sir John Reith, 16/11/1932. Reith, *Into the Wind.* Hodder & Stoughton, 1949, p. 164.

"I fear there is nothing to say . . ." Letter from Elgar to Basil Maine, 13/10/1932. CL, p. 805.

Page 79

". . . the Elgar business is finally fixed up . . ." Diary of Sir John Reith, 8/12/1932. BBC.

". . . a public administrator . . ." Letter from Bernard Shaw to *The Times*, 20/12/1932.

"There have been many instances of great men . . ." Cutting from an unidentified newspaper, Elgar Birthplace.

Page 80

". . . who remembered meeting him one evening . . ." Anecdote supplied by Nina Driver.

"At the Christmas of 1932 . . ." *Edward Elgar, The Record of a Friendship.* Burley and Carruthers, Barrie & Jenkins 1972, p. 204.

"The fact that Sir Edward Elgar . . ." Newspaper cuttings album, Elgar Birthplace.

Page 81

". . . he was able to complete another sketch . . ." See *Edward Elgar, the sketches for Symphony No. 3, elaborated by Anthony Payne,* Boosey & Hawkes full score, first movement, bars 234 – 243.

Page 82

"During the first half of 1933 . . ." EAF, p. 455.

Page 83

"He wrote his regrets . . ." See *Fenby on Delius,* S. Lloyd (ed.) Thames Publishing, 1996, pp. 123 & 125.

Page 84

". . . she had been gently warned . . ." Family information.

Page 85

". . . some sympathetic person . . ." Diary of Fred Gaisberg, 27/8/1933. Quoted in EoR, pp. 213 – 214.

Page 86

". . . Eric Fenby made his own independent approach . . ." S. Lloyd (ed.) *op. cit.,* p. 136.

"If I can't complete the Third Symphony . . ." CL, p. 819.

". . . he haltingly asked Billy Reed . . ." See Reed's *Elgar as I Knew Him*, Gollancz, 1973 pp. 114 – 115.

"He is greatly living in the most extraordinary dreams . . ." Letter from Carice Elgar-Blake to Ernest Newman, 28/1/1934. Quoted in CL, p. 822.

"I began to see visions of his ultimate recovery . . ." Reed, *op. cit.* , pp. 115 – 116.

Page 87

"And no 3rd. Symphony after all . . ." Letter from T. E. Lawrence to Carice Elgar Blake, 24/2/1934, in the possession of Raymond Monk.

Chapter Three Life Goes On

Page 102

". . . it will be one of the great moments . . ." Letter from Vaughan Williams to Edward Elgar, 19/2/ 1934. LoL, p. 480.

". . . I do want you to know . . ." Letter from Carice Elgar Blake to Vaughan Williams, 25/4/1934. WVW p. 377.

Page 103

". . . unashamed tears . . ." EAF, p. 467.

". . . Granville Bantock, for one, offered his services." Letter of 17/3/1968 from Adrian Boult to Carice Elgar Blake in possession of Raymond Monk.

Page 104

"What is a symphony?" Letter from Shaw to W. H. Reed, 17/8/1934. BS p. 378.

Page 105

"I was surprised at V. W. suddenly sticking his knife into me . . ." Letter of 20/1/1935 from Shaw to Arthur Troyte Griffith, *Ibid*, p. 397.

Page 106

For information concerning her father's life I am indebted to Sylvia Disley.

". . . quietly arranging to be known as Mrs Cheeseman." Information from Sylvia Disley and Nina Driver.

Page 107

". . . Don was an expert horologist . . ." According to his Obituary, ' . . . he spent a lifetime collecting and restoring clocks of all varieties, which he later donated to National Trust establishments all over Britain, and also to Universities and Government buildings throughout the world. One of his clocks is now in the Canberra Parliament building in Australia.'

Page 108

". . . it does seem to me a great safeguard . . ." Letter of 2/4/1939 from Carice Elgar Blake to Basil Maine. *Twang with our Music*, Basil Maine, The Epworth Press, 1957, p. 107.

". . . she had been left income but no capital . . ." The Will of Edward William Elgar, 2/1/1932, paragraph 7.

"Sir Edward Elgar told me in a recent letter . . ." Memorandum from Sir John Reith to Jardine Brown, 2/3/1934. BBC.

Page 109

"Lunched with Sir Hugh Allen . . ." Diary of Sir John Reith, 22/5/1933. BBC.

". . . lunched with Landon Ronald . . ." *Ibid.*, 25/1/1934. BBC.

". . . lunched with Ronald at the Langham . . ." *Ibid.*, 2/3/1934. BBC. Reith did not always move easily among musicians, although he was by no means unconscious of his effect on them. On one occasion he was present when Tertis and Harriet Cohen played at an Old Barts Students' dinner; 'both seemed pleased that I had spoken to them afterwards' he wrote, 'and said they were nervous playing before me.' After a performance of Elgar's First Symphony given by Ronald, Reith 'went to see him afterwards and he was very pleased.' He 'really much enjoyed' himself at a performance of *Belshazzar's Feast*, and was led to write that 'If I lived in town, I would go to concerts fairly regularly.' That evening he spoke to one of the composers afterwards, 'who was evidently very appreciative.' But one day Reith met his match. 'A dreadful visit from Dame Ethel Smythe, the most aggressive and tiring individual I think I know.' (Diary, 29/5/1933. BBC).

Page 110

"The Corporation for itself and its successors . . ." Agreement between the BBC and Carice Elgar Blake, 20/7/1934. BBC.

Page 112

"I am hoping that you have been able to enjoy the wonderful weather . . ." Letter from Elgar to Adela Schuster, 17/3/1933. LoL. , pp. 466 – 467.

Page 114

". . . something of the special symbolism of a national shrine." See *A Visit to Elgar's Birthplace,* Patric Stevenson, *Musical Times,* October 1942, pp. 297 – 299.

"When I first joined Carice . . ." *Carice Irene Blake: Memories, 1941-1970.* H. Sybil Wohlfeld, *Elgar Society Journal,* Vol. 6, No. 5, May 1990, pp. 8 – 9. Reprinted by kind permission of the Editor.

Page 116

"That horrible woman 'Dorabella' . . ." V-W's dislike of the person extended also to her music. 'I fear I cannot sympathise with "Dorabella's" effusions,' he wrote to Michael Kennedy in 1953. 'She seems to think that hers is the only variation, and to my mind it is the worst and weakest of the lot.' WVW, p. 383.

Page 117

"You cannot deplore your departure . . ." Letter from Bernard Shaw to Lord Reith, 25/2/ 1948. BS pp. 815 – 816.

Page 119

"The pension was a miracle of public recognition . . ." Letter from Bernard Shaw to Rutland Boughton, 28/5/1948. Quoted in Michael Hurd, *Immortal Hour, The Life and Period of Rutland Boughton,* Routledge & Kegan Paul, 1962, p. 120.

". . . this, as it stands . . ." Letter from Carice Elgar Blake to the *Sunday Times,* 27/5/ 1962.
Page 120
"I very much admired Vera . . ." Letter to the writer from Sylvia Disley, 19/4/2000
"I recall him telling me . . .' *Ibid.*
Page 121
"He told me . . ." *Ibid.*

Appendix. *' You'll never leave me, will you? '*

Page 132
". . . the illegitimate daughter . . ." See Michael Kennedy, *The Mysterious Mrs Nelson. Sunday Telegraph,* 15/11/1992.
Page 133
"*. . . ministered to him such sacraments as he could receive."* CL p. 823

INDEX

Abbey Road Studios 15, 32, 33
Adonais (Shelley) 6, 8-9
Albert Hall 16, 77
Alexander's Feast (Dryden) 36, 74
Allen, Sir Hugh 65, 109
As you came from the holy land
(Ralegh) xv-xvi, 73
Atkins, Ivor 6, 68, 86, 103, 110
  Wulstan 33, 65, 67, 68, 81, 82, 85, 103

Bach, J. S. 45
  Mass in B Minor 45
Bailey, P. J. (*Festus*) 36
Bantock, Granville 82, 103
BBC Symphony Orchestra 77
Beecham, Thomas 43, 106, 109, 120
Beethoven, L van 4, 35, 76, 84, 104
Berlioz, Hector 104
Berwick Sayers, W. C. 18, 137
Binyon, Laurence 2
Birchwood Lodge 39
Blake, Sam 40, 65, 70, 77-79, 82, 83,
110, 111, 113
Blom, Eric 116
Bonavia, Ferruccio 16, 67
Boughton, Rutland 118, 119
Boult, Adrian 16, 79, 109, 110
Brahms, Johannes 10, 20, 26, 45
  Requiem 10, 26, 45
  Symphony in D major 45
  Symphony in C Minor 45
Bridge, Frank vii
Brinkwells 1, 2, 111
Britten, Benjamin vii, 13
Brooke, Harold 3, 68, 69, 83
Brown, Jardine 79, 108
Brunskill, Muriel 70
Burley, Rosa v, 1, 80

Cheeseman, Don 106, 107, 111, 114,
120, 121

Clark, Lord 133
Clifford, Mary 42, 69, 85, 118, 130
Coates, John 31
Coleridge-Taylor, Samuel 15, 28
  Magnificat and Nunc Dimmittis in F
  28
Colles, H. C. 12
Colvin, Sidney 1, 11
Croydon vi, 15, 16, 19, 28, 34, 43, 44,
77, 83
  Advertiser 17, 19
  Baths Hall 27
  Sacred Harmonic Society 15
  Philharmonic Society 15, 16, 82,
  115
  Symphony Orchestra 15, 20, 27, 79
  Times 18, 28
  Triennial Festival 15, 17, 26
Crystal Palace 82

Daemon of the World, The (Shelley)
6-8
Daily Express 14
Daily Mail 76
Daily Telegraph 14, 80, 110
Davies, Walford 1
Delibes, Léo 45
Delius, Frederick 15, 83, 84, 86
de Navarro, Mary Anderson 9, 86
Dent, Professor E. J. vii, 11, 14
Desmond, Astra 83
Disley, Sylvia xii, 120, 139, 141, 143
Donalda, Pauline 20
Donne, John 5
Donnizetti, Gaetano 45
Dryden, John 36, 74

Elgar, Alice v, vii, x, xi, 1, 2, 10, 12, 23,
25, 39, 41, 85
Elgar, Ann 25, 41
Elgar and Poetry 70-76

Elgar Birthplace Museum 107, 110, 111, 114

Elgar, Carice (later Mrs Elgar Blake) vi, vii, xi, 2, 39-42, 64, 65, 67-69, 75, 77, 80, 81, 84-87, 102, 107, 108-111, 113, 114, 116, 118, 130, 132, 133

Elgar, Edward v, vi, vii and *passim*
  state of mind after wife's death 1-2, unconventional behaviour 2-3, religious thinking 3-4, 5, 9, 11, 12, suggests Shelley settings for Wcr Fest 6-9, relationship with Shaw 9-12, 117-119, Baronetcy 14, opens Abbey Road Studios 15, arrives at Croydon 18-19, wish to marry Vera 24, meets V 1st time 28, meets V at Reeds' party 30-31, discusses interpretations of Gerontius 31, invites V to lunch at Langham 33, discusses poetry with V 35, 36, 42, 70-74, discusses music with V 35, 38, 41, 45, 46, 70-72, 75, invites V to Marl Bank 36, plays Vln Sonata with V at Marl Bank 37-38, meets V at Carlton Hill flat 39-43, arranges with V to exchange letters through Carice 42, reasons for continuing relationship with V 43, introduces V to Adela Schuster 45, gives V sketches of Vln Sonata 47, resumption of creative energy 65, sends joke score to Dulcie 66, filmed with V at Marl Bank, shows her Birthplace 69, writes to V of Menuhin recording 75, signs BBC contract for Sym 3 77, uncertainty over completion of Sym 76, 77, 80, 81, 75th birthday concerts 77-79, sends V Sym sketches 81, signs of illness 81, 83-85, flies to Paris 83, conducts Sym 2 last time, behaviour at 1933 Hford Fest 85, cancer discovered, asks that no one should tinker with

Sym 86, dies 87, 134, final weeks 130-134, conducts *Caractacus* excerpts 131-132, funeral 134.
Arthur music 2
Beau Brummel 2
The Apostles 1, 11, 16, 82, 83, 107, 115
Caractacus 2, 86, 130
Cello Concerto 1, 86 (arrgt. for viola)
Civic Fanfare 2
Cockaigne Overture 78
Dream of Gerontius, The vi, 6, 14, 15, 17, 26, 27, 29-31, 68, 77, 80, 85, 102-104, 107, 111
'Enigma' 71
Enigma Variations 9, 71, 78-80
For the Fallen 15, 68
Introduction and Allegro 74
Kingdom, The 15, 16, 79, 86, 103, 115
King Olaf 77
Land of Hope and Glory 15, 32
Last Judgement, The 6, 65
Light of Life, The 15, 27
Music Makers, The 16, 67, 68, 70, 71, 76
'Nimrod' 9, 71, 72, 114
Nursery Suite 14, 38
Piano Concerto v, 24, 65
Piano Quintet 11, 69
Pomp and Circumstance Marches, 74. No. 5 in C Major, 13
Salut d'amour 66
Severn Suite 13, 65, 68
Spanish Lady, The v, 24, 65, 78, 81, 85
String Quartet 32
Symphony No 1, v, 43, 68
Symphony No 2, vii, 7, 14, 25, 26, 65, 72, 78, 85, 87, 103
Symphony No 3 (see also under Payne, Tony) vi, vii, x, 9, 11, 24, 44,

65, 67, 76, 77, 79, 81, 83-87, 102-104, 107, 109, 110, 117, 121
'V. H.'s Own Theme' v, 24, 81
Violin Concerto v, 1, 14, 65, 68, 74, 75, 77, 78, 83, 87, 107
Violin Sonata vi, 36-38, (*Romance* 38) 46-47, 111, 139
Elgar's Last Muse (film) xii
Elwes, Gervase 31
Epipsychidion (Shelley) 75-76 107

Fenby, Eric 15, 83, 86
Fischer, Sarah 20
Forbes, Norman 65
Forsyte Saga, The 138
Franck, César 15

Gaisberg, Fred 84, 85
Grafton, Madge 38
Grant's (Croydon) 18, 25
Grieg, Edvard 15
Griffith, Arthur Troyte 10, 64, 69, 105
Griller Quartet 69

Harrison, Kathleen vii, 130, 131, 133, 134
Haydn, Joseph 104
Hess, Myra 20, 69
Hobday, Ethel 20
Hockman, Dulcie vi, 21-23, 44, 46, 65, 67, 80, 82, 84-86, 111, 117, 120, 133
Hockman, John 21, 44, 85, 139
Hockman, Joseph vi, 21, 22
Hockman, Vera (later known as Cheeseman)
   v, x, xi and *passim*. Personality and background 20-24, marriage 21, meets E for first time 28, meets E at Reeds' party 30-31, meets E at Langham Hotel 34, meets E at Marl Bank and plays Vln Sonata 37, friendship and meetings with Carice 40, 67, 68, 77-79, 82-86, 111, 113,

meets E at Carlton Hill flat 41-43, attends Beecham First Symphony perf. 43-44, attends Wcr Festival 1932 as member of E's house party 68-70, filmed with E at Marl Bank 69, visits E Birthplace cottage 69, 107, warned over relationship with E 84, attends Hfd Festival 1933 with mother 85, destruction of her letters to E 87, 121, plays in VW *Gerontius* perf 102, sends VW words for setting 103, meets Don Cheeseman 106, joins ARP and suffers accident to head 114, adopts daughter 114, seeks publication of Elgarian memoirs 115-116, illness and death 119-121.
Writings:
Elgar and Poetry 70-76, 114
The Story of November 7th, 1931 vi, xi, 24-25, 26-47, 69, 106
Holmes, Sherlock 14
Holst, Gustav 103
Hurlstone, William 15
Hyperion (associated with Longfellow story) vi, 29, 32, 39, 41, 42, 45-47, 87, 107, 114
Hurd, Michael 119

Inglis, Hazel 21, 27

Jackson, Barry 12
Jaeger, August Johannes 9, 80, 81

Keats, John 8
Kennedy, Daisy 20
Kennedy, Michael xii
Kirby, Alan 15-18, 107, 115

Lacey, Canon T. A. 4-6, 28
Lambert, Constant 2, 15
Langham Hotel 32, 33, 35, 40, 45, 70, 77-79, 82, 85, 109

Lawrence, T. E. (Lawrence of Arabia, also known as Shaw, T. E.) x, 68, 75, 87
Lee Williams, Dr C 2, 3
Legge, Walter 67
Leicester, Hubert 3
   Nella 113
   Philip 3, 113
Leith Hill Festival 21, 102
Listener, The 107, 109, 110
Liszt, Franz 104
London Symphony Orchestra 15, 20, 27, 30, 43, 86, 115

MacDonald, Ramsay v, 117
Maine, Basil 2, 14, 77, 84-86, 108, 116
Malvern Festival   11, (1929), 111 (1937)
Mansfield Evans , Captain 39
Marco 31, 37, 38, 46, 67
Marks, Amy (also Joseph) 20
Marl Bank vii, 25, 33, 36, 37, 46, 64, 65, 68, 70, 74-76, 81, 84, 86, 87, 111, 114, 130, 131, 133
Marlowe, Christopher 42
Marvell, Andrew 73
Mendelssohn, Felix 85
   Elijah 85
Menuhin, Yehudi 15, 68, 74, 75, 77, 83
Messiah 15, 69, 115
Meyerbeer, Giacomo 45
Mina 37, 38, 46, 67
Mobey 67
Moore Ede, Dean of Worcester 6, 7, 131
Moore Ede, son of above, Elgar's doctor 131, 134
Moore, J. N. x
Moiseivitch, Benno 20
Musical Times 16, 116
Music and Letters 11, 104, 116

Nash, Heddle 31
Newman, Cardinal 1, 8
   The Dream of Gerontius (poem) 1, 8

Newman, Ernest vii, 4, 11, 64-65
Norbury, Florence v
Noyes, Alfred 73

Observer, The 69
O'Shaughnessy, Arthur 70

Parry, Sir Hubert 18, 71, 105
   Blest Pair of Sirens 18
Payne, Tony v, 104, 121, 140
   Edward Elgar the Sketches for Symphony No 3 elaborated by, v, x, 104, 121, 140
Pearson, Hesketh 11
Penny, Dora (*Dorabella,* later Mrs Richard Powell) v, vi, 1, 116
Pinza, Ezio 38
Pollitzer, Adolphe 31
Pownall, David xii
   Elgar's Third xii
Promenade Concerts 13-14, 26, 85
Prowse, Keith 67, 79

Queen's Hall 13, 14, 15, 25, 43, 85
Queen Mab (Shelley) 7

Ralegh, Sir Walter xvi, 73
Reed, W. H. xi, 12, 15, 19-21, 26-30, 32, 34, 65, 68, 69, 79, 81-86, 103, 107, 108, 110, 111, 115, 118, 132
   James (Mrs Reed) 34, 79, 82-84, 111
Reith, Sir John (later Lord) vii, 76, 77, 79, 81, 86, 108-110, 117, 118, 142
Robin Hill 21, 24, 67, 70, 77-79, 82-84, 103, 106, 111, 114, 138
Ronald, Landon 77, 79, 80, 82, 83, 86, 108-110
Rossini, Giacomo 104
Royal Academy of Music 16
Royal College of Music xi, 45, 67, 70, 106
Royal Philharmonic Orchestra 106, 120

Royal Philharmonic Society 16
Russell, Sybil 114

Sammons, Albert 20, 78
Sargent, Malcolm 16
Scharrer, Irene 20, 22
Schumann, Robert 35, 64
Schuster, Adela v, 44, 45, 112
   Frank, 44
Severn House 1, 11
Shaw, Charlotte 87, 111
Shaw, Bernard v, vii, x, xi, xii, 9-12, 14,
45, 77, 79, 85, 102, 103, 105, 117-119.
Lends Elgar £1000 64, presses   for
Third Symphony 64, 67, 76, 84
   Admirable Bashville, The 9
   Apple Cart, The 11
   Devil's Disciple, The 10
   Doctor's Dilemma, The 10
   You Never Can Tell 10
Shaw, Mr & Mrs 68, 75, 84
Shaw, T. E. see Lawrence, T. E.
Shelley, Percy Bysshe 6-9, 28, 71, 75,
107
Shirley Park Hotel 21, 31, 33, 44, 45,
47,139
Sinclair, George Robertson 5
Smythe, Dame Ethel 142
South Bank Nursing Home 86, 113,
130, 131, 133
Stanford, Sir Charles 18, 105
   Songs of the Sea 18
Story of November 7th, 1931, The vi,
xi, 24, 25, 26-47, 69, 106
Strauss, Richard 15, 72, 104
Stuart Wortley, Alice v, 1
   Clare 113
Sunday Times, The 119

Tertis, Lionel 86
Three Choirs Festivals
   Gloucester (1931) 14, (1934) 103

Hereford (1891) 5, (1897) 5, (1927)
2, (1933) 85, (1936) 111
   Worcester (1926) 4, (1929) 6, (1932)
67, 68, 70, 76 (1935) 107
Times, The 12, 16, 79, 109
Tovey, Donald 82
Trinity College of Music 16

Vandervelde, Lalla 10
Vaughan Williams, Adeline 111
Vaughan Williams, Ralph xi, 15, 18, 21,
24-26, 102-105, 107, 110-113, 115-
117, 138
   Dona Nobis Pacem 112
   Hugh the Drover 115, 116
   Sea Symphony 18, 107
   Symphony No. 4 112
   Symphony No. 5 116
   Three Mystical Songs 21, 138
Verdi, Guiseppe 10, 14, 38, 79, 111
   Falstaff 79
   Requiem 10, 38, 111

Wagner, Richard 4-6, 10, 17, 35, 38, 79,
104
Mastersinger Prelude 38
Parsifal 4, 5, 79
Walton, William 133
Weaver, Helen v
Whitman, Walt 3
Wilbur, Jay 12
Wilde, Oscar 44
Willcocks, Sir David xi
Wilson, Steuart xi, 82, 116
Wood, Henry 13, 15, 17, 18
Worcester Daily Times 4-6
Worthington, Julia v, 1

Yeats, W. B. 20